Foreword

Man is a complex being. When one area of his life is out of balance, it affects other areas. Spiritual problems cause psychological problems, which may cause physical problems. This book shows what can happen in a person's life when he fails to recognize all that he has in Christ. The case histories which Dr. Little presents in *The Christian and Emotional Problems* forcibly prove how failure to understand and live the victorious Christian life affects every aspect of a person's being.

The concluding chapter, written by Theodore H. Epp, tells how every believer may have a victorious life. When Christians realize they have been freed from sin's control so they no longer have to sin, it revolutionizes their lives. However, the sin nature will usurp control over the believer if he does not follow God's directions for victorious living. But when the directions are followed, the effects are seen not only in triumphant Christian living but also in mental and physical well-being.

—Harold J. Berry
Literature Editor

Preface

It is obvious that a book this size could not consider all the emotional problems of Christians. Therefore, if the reader searches for a facsimile of his specific problem in this book he may not find it. In particular, this book deals with problems which my Christian patients have most often presented to me.

The chapter on "self" will undoubtedly give anyone with an emotional problem a good clue for the basis of his problem. It will also help him to understand that if self has not been reckoned to be crucified, dead and buried with Christ, he will become a maladjusted Christian with emotional problems. The concluding chapter of this book, written by Theodore H. Epp, will be of special help in aiding the reader's understanding of what it means to be dead to sin, but alive unto God.

The purpose of this book is to help the Christian with emotional problems to turn back to the Bible—away from man's reasoning—and not try to solve his problems by worldly diversions.

Meditating on the Word of God is not merely diverting the mind; it is fellowship with God.

There is a wide range of Christian profession. Most of my patients say they are Christians, but it seems to me that sometimes their psychiatric histories cast a shadow over their testimonies. However, I am not the patient's judge. I am his physician. As the patient's physician I try to find the cause of his conflicts and suffering by psychotherapy.

Psychiatry is a specialized branch of medicine which deals with diseases of the mind. Christian psychiatry reaches down into the soul and treats the whole man—spirit, soul and body.

—L. Gilbert Little, M.D.

Contents

Chapter 1

Self-Centered Christians

The Christian who remains in the carnal state is self-centered, bound to "self," and suffers from too much self. This chapter will include excerpts from my case histories, which show the conflicts and the consequent suffering of self-centered Christians. Succeeding chapters will show how self is involved in the problems of nervous Christians; how self dominates the life and the works of carnal Christians; how self breaks the Christian's fellowship with God; how Satan—the master strategist—plans his attack on the Christian according to the susceptibility of self in the Christian; and how self is unmasked in the psychotherapy room.

When a new babe is born into God's kingdom, he is still in Satan's domain, surrounded by his atmosphere of evil-influencing powers. Satan's forces subtly attack the babe in Christ, trying to hinder his growth and, if at all possible, stop his growth entirely. If the Christian babe has not buried the old self in Christ, turned from it, and

9

turned to his new Object—Christ Jesus—Satan will keep him self-centered.

A 34-year-old woman said, "I have been a Christian for 11 years. It seems to me that I was baptized more from a desire to obey the command to be baptized, rather than from a sign of a new life within. I am afraid I did not really see myself as a sinner, and I do not think I was really converted at the time. My legalistic pattern of life is most miserable. I have made conscience my guide. I need to commit myself to Christ, but seemingly I cannot. I seem to be bound with an iron chain that I cannot let God break. The wonderful spiritual blessings seem not for me to grasp. Could there be something wrong with me mentally? One psychiatrist said that I have not matured emotionally. He was not a Christian; he did not understand my problem."

As is the case in the lives of so many Christians, when this patient could not control her thoughts she feared a mental condition, which prompted her to go to a psychiatrist. The non-Christian psychiatrist, not understanding the things of the Spirit, sought out psychological factors of the old nature to treat. Since he could not point her to Christ, she became more involved with her old nature—self—which only strengthened her legalistic attitude.

This patient continued, "I am afraid my mind will attach onto something I can't drop. This started way back when I tried to force evil thoughts out of my mind. I determined to have a clean mind. I wrestled with the thoughts until I found myself thinking only on the undesirable thoughts that I abhorred. I made myself ill by wrong thinking. The psychiatrist said he was trying to reeducate me; but really, all he was doing was trying to get my mind to reach out to new thoughts. But I always soon found something to worry about."

Later, when this patient had found peace and joy in her mind and in her soul, she testified: "It was only when I learned to turn my thoughts from myself to the Bible and have my daily time with the Lord that I broke this spell [Satan's power over her thoughts and over self]."

Down through the centuries Satan has urged his subjects to reason out problems for themselves. He has urged them to prove to their own satisfaction that they are self-sustaining and do not need to look to a higher power. This is rebellion against God.

As we look about us we see that Satan's subjects work out a religious, moral standard of their own in which they trust for salvation. It has become their idol and, like all idols, its power controls and binds them.

Quite often Christian babes do not turn from their religious, moral self-idol. They may receive Christ as Saviour but continue to be controlled by their idol. They have not desired to take Christ as the Object of their lives. Until the Holy Spirit awakens them to desire the "sincere milk of the word" and to search the Scriptures for themselves,

11

they will be governed by disconnected statements from the Bible, statements taken out of context, which go to make up their idol.

The Christian who does not put on the Lord Jesus Christ and make Him the Object of his life is bound to suffer from emotional problems. There is an inner conflict caused by Satan and the old self warring against the Holy Spirit, who came into the Christian babe to teach him to turn to his new Object, Jesus Christ, for his life. When this Christian reads the Bible or is under the influence of other Christians, his old self-standard becomes a stumbling block to him. Moral self being his object, not Christ, he produces works of self which do not give peace to the soul. He has no fruit of the Spirit, no joy, no peace, no fellowship with God.

Self-Control

Some counselors urge Christians to use self-control and not to blame Satan for their acts of misconduct. To the self-centered Christian this too often suggests using more willpower in the matter of conduct. The individual turns more and more to his self-control. This is exactly what pleases Satan. As long as Satan can bind the individual to self as his object he can control him.

The Christian can only overcome Satan when he turns from all of self and has Christ Jesus as his Object, for "we are more than conquerors through him that loved us" (Rom. 8:37). But most nervous

Christians are like the patient who said, "I try to control myself by myself."

"When someone tells me to trust the Lord," said a patient, "I keep on trying. Then I wonder if I am trying hard enough, until my thoughts are too much on the doubt."

Later this man testified: "My wife and I have studied the verses which tell of the effect of Jesus' shedding His blood. This certainly gets me calmed down. I then think on what Christ did for me, and I seem to realize I am trusting but not making an effort to trust."

"I have so much pride," confessed a patient. "I would not want anybody to know I study the Bible so much. I have always believed such people were weak. I believed it was a matter of willpower. All the preaching I ever heard stressed controlling your thoughts from evil, which made me believe the Bible readers were just reading it to divert their minds."

It does not help the emotional patient if we map out a diversionary program but do not get at the root of his problem. And getting at the root of the Christian's problem will not give him peace if he does not establish a proper relationship with Christ.

A patient who had turned back to self and self-control said, "I read a book by a noted evangelist who wrote that it is up to you to keep sin out of your life. Before that time I went by grace, just keeping my mind on Christ. That statement seemed to turn me back to myself again.

13

I wondered if I was really saved, because I was not perfect enough. Then I worried about my sins and imperfections until Satan had me praying to God for my many sins that were under the blood long ago."

Another patient who suffered from a compulsion to control self said, "I have a feeling I must go on and overcome it. But what if I can't! Then where will I be? When I get tense I concentrate on it to keep it under control. That makes me more tense. I get so tense I am afraid I will eventually blank out and do something crazy in front of all the people. Then they will think I am a mental case. This makes me panicky. Panic is dead-end feeling."

At "dead-end feeling" the patient is completely absorbed in himself, completely dominated by self, and is utterly helpless against his self.

In this psychological era Satan is battling for the minds of men. He can only battle for the Christian's mind when the Christian takes his attention off his Object, Jesus Christ, and turns it back to his self-nature. It is only the Christians who have gone through severe trials and finally have been able to overcome self and keep their eyes on Christ who recognize that their battle was with Satan.

A nervous Christian who was making an effort in his self-will to resist his fantasies said, "I seem to have to pull myself out of myself and my fantasies. If I try to force myself away from my fantasies I seem to be keeping my thoughts on the problem that I want to dispel. By keeping my mind on the resistance I put up against the problem, it finally binds all my thoughts on the resistance."

Satan has this patient bound to his self. Surely we must resist the Devil, but self cannot do it. James 4:7 says, "Submit yourselves therefore to God." In other words, we are to have our eyes on the Lord. Then we will not have to worry about watching our conduct or resisting fantasies. The love of God in us will have us turn our thoughts on Him.

A Sunday school teacher said, "I had to keep my mind on trying to keep myself from fainting and from the feelings in the back of my head and from my palpitation. While I was teaching the young people's class in our church my mind was divided. Then I scared myself more by wondering what I would do if I got worse."

Many others in similar situations complain of "splitting" in their minds—one half is absorbed in the work at hand; while the other half is wondering what the public is able to see about them that is peculiar. As one such worried patient said, "I was looking at myself while singing in the choir, wondering if others could see that my mind was on myself, and wondering if I was still acting conventional."

It is not unusual to find churches and various Christian and religious organizations buzzing with activities of nervous Christians who are energized by the self-nature. They are busy doing "works" for the Lord, not bringing forth the fruit of the

15

Spirit, but the fruits of self. Satan has them deluded into believing that God will bless their works; that if they work for the Lord He will deliver them from their fears; that their good works will "deliver them in the days of their transgressions."

Self-centered Christians desire the peace and joy of spiritual Christians, but they do not realize that joy in the Lord does not come forth by much religious exercise. Peace and joy come through the Spirit within.

Satan's Hindering Spirit

"I seem to have a hindering spirit," said a seminary student who hesitated to continue his preparation for the ministry because he had periodic attacks of anxiety. He believed he would be a poor example behind a pulpit without victory over Satan.

"For several years," continued the patient, "I believed my fear panics were sent from God to make me repent and be delivered from my past sins. I thought the Lord was trying to make me live holy. All the years I was bound to this fear I never once suspected this was the working of Satan. Every time I masturbated, or was sorely tempted, I had a fear of punishment from God. I was convinced that I had not been forgiven previously and thoroughly cleansed, or else I would not be tempted. I know I John 1:9, but somehow Satan had me blinded to the meaning. Once I understood

16

this, I saw how Satan was making me pray for past sins already under the blood. When I trusted the Lord for forgiveness and thanked Him for His atoning work on Calvary for me, these panics became less frequent and were of shorter duration."

A Bible school graduate suffering from confused thoughts said, "I don't have victory in my Christian life. I lack assurance of forgiveness. It all started over masturbation. I can't resist temptation. I feel so defeated. I have pain in here [pointed to heart]. When I cry real hard, it helps.

"When I read the Bible or pray, there are so many interruptions. Sounds and thoughts come in. It wears me out and hurts in my heart. There is a hindering spirit that wants to come into my mind. It is most annoying when I read my Bible, pray or sit in church. It got worse after my doctor told me to read a popular religious book. He was not a Christian, but he thought he was helping me."

The symptoms of which this patient complained were caused by her forced effort to divert her mind by Bible reading and prayer. There was no fellowship in reading God's Word, but a psychological attempt at diversion. When she understood the true meaning of meditating on God's Word she was able to gain assurance.

A patient who was hindered by a spirit of pride came to me with these words: "The doctors say my trouble is mental, but I know it is the work of Satan. God is working in me to clean up my life. I have had an exalted opinion of my ability. I have

17

expected the church to use me. I thought they should receive me with open arms. That, I know now, was self-exaltation."

A 65-year-old Christian gave this testimony of his suffering at the hand of Satan: "At the age of 12 I received Christ as my Saviour. I had joy and was happy in the Lord for several years. Then I was suddenly terribly shocked. I had a sudden urge to cut my throat with a knife after I had a fear that I was rejected by God for some sin which seemed to isolate me—cut me off from God. For years I had these periods of oppressive gloom. Doctors diagnosed them as cycles of depression. I feel this was satanic. At least I recognized it as from Satan and always turned to God, thanking Him for what He did for me. Then the fear would leave me for a season. These periods of gloom don't last as long as they used to—only a few days. Then I am free until the Devil tries to make an issue of some sin."

"If I think on Calvary I can sleep," said a woman. "Any other Bible thought will not put me to sleep. It seems those are the only verses that have power over Satan. I want to yield and serve the Lord. I want to get rid of my sins. When I read other verses, my mind seems to recall my past sins. Satan seems to parade them all past my mind's eye as if I am not entirely free of my past sins. In that way I build up doubt and more doubt until I do not feel saved. Where do I go from here?"

Where should the patient go from here? Where indeed should this nervous Christian go to get away from the hindering spirit of Satan? Where, but back to Calvary, and there remember what Christ did for her; that past sins have been removed "as far as the east is from the west." There Satan will lose his power to parade her past sins before her and hinder her from serving the Lord.

Spiritual Christians recognize the hindering spirit and turn to the Lord for an understanding of their conflicts. However, many Christians are so imbued with the psychological thinking of the world that they do not recognize the hindering spirit of Satan, and they turn to the world for an answer to their problems. This leaves them bound to self, just where Satan wants them.

Many Christians tell me that they spent years consulting psychiatrists who deal with emotional problems from the non-Christian viewpoint. In the meantime they may attend church or be occupied with religious activities. This shows that the Holy Spirit has not given them up to their self. Even while they rebel against God, the Holy Spirit keeps them God-conscious. But others finally resort to tranquilizers to deaden the "still small voice." The following confession is an example:

"Now I have gone so far I don't even feel the spiritual struggle. I am taken up with my self-thoughts. I just can't grasp the spiritual struggle. I am seared, or numbed, to spiritual thoughts. I seem to know there is something I want, but I do not have enough willpower to struggle against or to get out of the cobweb. I feel somewhat like the fly in a spider's web that has been stung and paralyzed and is waiting to be devoured at some later time. I am not dead; I am very much alive. I am anxious and tense. I have no further ideas regarding life than that I am trapped.

"I was born again at a revival but at the time I was attending a modern church and did not grow to love the Word. I tried to keep myself saved by my right living. I could not keep up with the standard I had set for myself. I got tense and anxious and cared less for the Word and God's people until"—a pause, and then—"so here I am."

And where is the patient? He is trapped in Satan's grip—trapped by Satan's hindering spirit. He needs someone to help him see that only Christ can release him from the trap.

Deceived by Hindering Spirits

Christians who seek an experience, a feeling or a sign to assure themselves of salvation and sins forgiven grow more and more into self. They are looking within for a sensation. A patient who had passed the initial joy of salvation said, "I felt so good right after I was saved. I had a feeling of ecstasy. When that left me, I worried about my salvation because I wanted so to keep that ecstasy. This 'dead' feeling makes me wonder if I am still saved. I was reared to place salvation on works. Now I catch myself and say, 'Wait a minute. You are saved by faith.' "

But the patient's faith was in her "feeling of ecstasy" which she believed was given her by God. Her assurance of salvation was based on this

20

feeling, not upon her faith in the shed blood of Christ. It was in her feeling rather than in believing. The spirit of ecstasy hindered her from immediately putting her trust in God. When this spirit had left her, there was only the "dead" feeling in its place.

Later, when this patient had put her trust completely in the Lord, she testified: "Your feelings can let you down."

Feelings are not proof of salvation. The ungodly do not "feel" lost.

A certain deacon of a church related this experience: "While standing next to the evangelist during opening prayer, I purposed in my heart to follow him closely, sentence by sentence. He prayed for an outpouring of the Spirit on the congregation. He asked for the outpouring of the Spirit on the saved to awaken them to a fruit-ful life. I prayed for this to come on me. My thoughts drifted to my anticipations for bodily feelings—which I did get. It started on my scalp and flowed through my body. I even had a slight sexual tingling. When prayer was ended I had no joy. I was left disgusted and dead to the message that followed. I just had no part in it. I thought I did, but I prayed in the flesh. The Devil fooled me."

It seems that these feelings of disgust, no joy, and futility are strong convictions that follow immediately after these Christians have ended their prayers which were controlled by the Devil. The state of these deceived Christians in bondage to

Satan is that they are closed in to self, completely self-centered. They are not happy in their states. But it is as many Christians who are tortured by hindering spirits, and have no peace of mind and soul, write and say, "I don't want to be this way. But how to get out of this trap!"

The Christian who wears the whole armor of God and is thoroughly instructed in righteousness will be able to discern the difference in the spirits. He knows that the Holy Spirit comes quietly and calms the spirit with peace and joy; whereas evil spirits come suddenly, playing on bodily sensations and drawing the patient's entire attention to self.

Hindering spirits keep nervous Christians in bondage to the old self-nature so they can be treated by the remedies of this world. Then Satan feels he has scored a victory. In a certain sense he has, because the self-centered Christian is unfruitful.

The hindering spirit of feeling has terrific power over the Christian once Satan gets the Christian to depend on his feelings. The problem with these nervous Christians is that Satan has them blinded to their error. After they have established a pattern of self-hypnotism they go from feeling to feeling.

One Christian patient made the following statements: "I doubt my salvation because I have no feelings to prove it. When they asked me, 'Do you have peace?' I said, 'No,' because I did not have a right feeling. I try to get rid of this feeling and to put a happy feeling into myself, but I feel hindered. When I get depressed or feel condemned, I wonder what sin I did today. I try to live perfectly before God and the church as well as I know how. If no one compliments me on it, I feel worthless. I decided on a hobby to give me ambition. Something that made me feel I was a success in the world. That did not last either. You can't be winning all the time."

No, the Christian who depends on his feelings can't win any of the time, because he is hindered by a spirit of doubt.

Fear of Having Self Dethroned

Some patients just cannot bear to have their ego—their self—dethroned. They may be unhappy and suffering, yet they fear the change that treatment might bring about. Not all patients who go to the psychiatrist plan to take his advice, or anyone else's for that matter. They are engaged in a battle to frustrate, deceive, and eventually defeat the counselor as they longed to defeat their parents during childhood and adolescence. With this immature, hostile attitude they seem determined to defeat even God. Since they have refused to be subservient to any authority, they will not read and study God's Word lest they become convicted.

One patient said, "When you are explaining something to me I am anxiously figuring out what I want to say to you. I am afraid perhaps you did not fully understand what I mean. I feel it is a sign of intelligence to be able to come up with a contradictory thought. I don't want you to feel superior to me." I have had several patients offer this explanation for their inability to grasp what was said. Some have admitted: "When you write me a letter explaining my problem, I seem to grasp it. I have time to think it over. I read your letter several times on different days. I seem to think more earnestly about what you are trying to get across to me because I can't argue with you."

Many patients, even Christians, are in the habit of listening to what is being said, not to absorb it, but to evaluate it to see if it condemns them. If they think it condemns them, they think and reason to themselves how to give a striking rebuttal not only to silence the speaker but also to reaffirm their own way of life.

A guilty Christian, in bondage to self, confessed how she tried to deceive the all-wise God: "I used to read *True Story* magazines. I knew I shouldn't do it. Then I would meditate on the stories. I felt guilty toward my husband—what if he knew I was thinking of love with other men? I used to read my Bible just enough to say I read my Bible every day. I did not remember what I read because my mind was filled with those stories. I felt guilty but not guilty enough to quit it."

This patient did not come to me for an understanding of her emotional problem. She hoped to receive a "better" tranquilizer to add to the three different brands she was already taking three times a day and at bedtime.

Drugs have their place in medicine. Even tranquilizers may be valuable aids, but by themselves they do not cure. Many patients on tranquilizers suffer from psychic heaviness. Anxiety may be curbed, but natural alertness and eagerness have somehow been suppressed. Often there is a sense of remoteness in the soul of the Christian overshadowed by tranquilizers. Once he may have testified that Christ was his all-in-all, and he may still testify that he is saved. But he no longer has the close, warm fellowship with Christ that he once had.

It could well be that fogging the mind by means of tranquilizers is a subtle method Satan has of bringing peace of mind. But what of the soul?

The following is a sincere heart confession of a Christian schizophrenic in a state of remission: "While you are talking I form pictures of what you say. I get so absorbed in my mental pictures I lose all track of what you are explaining. I lose the last part of your explanation. Since I have been a little confused, it is hard to control my thoughts. It is so easy for my mind to make pictures or imaginations. I have learned since I got over my mental illness to cast down my imaginations as soon as they start. I got sick because I enjoyed them."

A very self-centered individual who does not want to part with self and imaginations said, "I keep my thoughts on myself even while people are talking to me. I won't let my thoughts go off myself. I don't want to hear people talk. I wish they would stay away. Their talking confuses my thoughts. It gives me a headache."

What fellowship can such self-centered Christians have with people who are rejoicing in the Lord? To say the least, it can only increase their suffering, but they do not recognize this suffering as being under the power of Satan. They consider their symptoms to be manifestations of a psychiatric problem, which makes them turn to psychiatry and the world instead of to daily nourishment from the Word of God. They may try to find some comfort in reading daily devotional books, but these are not a substitute for the Bible. The power to heal, cleanse and comfort is in the Word of God.

Chapter 2

Too Self-Centered to Get Well

The self-centered Christian cannot get well because he cannot will to see anything but self. He has set up a mental block which bars entrance of anything that would enlighten him in regard to his conflict.

One patient said, "When you go to explain something to me, I listen attentively to what you commence to say. Then I have a frightening thought enter my mind that says, 'What if you can't comprehend what is being said? Maybe your mind is not able to grasp it.' Then more fear comes into my mind. Next, I am all absorbed in my feelings. That is why I only hear the first part of what you say. My feelings and thoughts become more important to me than what you say. I just do not hear the last part of what you say."

During psychotherapy this patient's history revealed that he regularly gave liberal offerings to a gospel broadcast and took delight in receiving long personal letters from the radio pastor. Yet he would not attend Sunday school with his family for fear he might be called upon to read a verse

27

from the Sunday school leaflet in the presence of the whole class. He attended church, but he made himself as inconspicuous as possible lest someone might call upon him to lead in prayer. Here is a paradox. He wanted to be noticed and was offended when the leaders of the church did not give him recognition for his liberality in tithes and offerings, which he thought should merit consideration from them. He expressed resentment at not being elected to the church board.

His attendance at church became irregular. His excuse was that he was too tired from duties of secular work; but he was hoping that someone would call on him and urge him to come to church with his family. This would assure him that they still loved him. In his moods of self-pity he toyed with the idea of going to another church, but refrained because of his family.

This man takes little interest in Bible reading. He may listen to his wife read the Bible, but he does not take an active part in the daily devotions with his family. He imitates other Christians, but spiritual growth is hindered because he appropriates only a few biblical facts that appeal to his vanity.

His self-standard of religious pride bids him draw a line of separation from the world where his moral conduct is concerned. He refrains from drinking alcoholic beverages, smoking and using profanity. In business he is honest to the point of scrupulosity. Even though he separates himself from what is worldly, he lacks a Christian

28

testimony. He does not confess with his mouth the Lord Jesus, and his self-works suggest religious fanaticism to the world. He exalts the fruits of self instead of the fruit of the Spirit.

What seems to be characteristic of Christians of this type is that they have momentary joy when first saved. They seem to receive the Word gladly, but they do not seem to relish the taste of the "sincere milk of the word" or crave more of this spiritual food. As if they had not tasted and found that He is good, they do not read the Bible to learn about the wonderful Saviour who redeemed them.

They desire to be numbered with the Christians for the sake of fellowship. As they go along they absorb a little Bible knowledge, which condemns them rather than bringing peace to their souls. They do not look to the Bible as the source of power for the Christian.

A nervous Christian woman, bound to her self-conscious feelings, suffered when in fellowship with other Christians. As is typical of such individuals, she tried to find a place in church where she could not be observed by others. She said, "I concentrate on all my bodily sensations, wondering if they can increase to the point where others might see I am nervous. I want to be where they can't see me all the time.

"I told my doctor it made me nervous to go to church. He said, 'Don't go then. You don't have to go to church. Not everybody goes to church.'

"If I don't go to church the people look at me, wondering what is wrong with me. I am afraid of what the people will say to me if I don't go. I was told by one of the church sisters, 'You are foolish; just get those ideas out of your head.'

"Then I try because I am afraid people will not like me if I continue in my worry. I can't go on without their love, so I try to please them by trying to control my thoughts. Then it seems I get into more trouble. I am aware of myself and watch my thoughts to see if I am keeping those undesirable worry thoughts out. The more I watch myself, the more aware I become of my worry thoughts.

"I am sure that people build up their own awareness. You exaggerate the symptoms you imagine you are going to have. You finally dwell on the thoughts moment by moment."

A self-centered Christian, who concentrated on her physical symptoms, became so involved with her various symptoms that she completely blocked out her convictions—which really were the basis for her suffering.

She explained her convictions thus: "Any bodily sensation that is new, abnormal or strange worries me until I find out what causes it. When the doctors don't seem sure of the diagnosis I am afraid they don't know. I must be certain. If the doctors are not certain, I wonder if I have something that can't be cured. I go to any length to find out what is wrong. I try every lab test that is conceivable to find out the cause of the trouble."

This patient required psychiatric help because she almost always had an anxiety urge concerning death after a visit from her mother. She tolerated her because she was her mother, but she could not love her because she had learned as a child that her mother's love was not sincere. Therefore, she spurned her mother's gifts and gestures of love. She had a subconscious sense of guilt because as a Christian she should love her mother. She was "afraid of death and going into outer darkness." She would shed tears of self-pity, but she could not sorrow to repentance.

Nervous Christians who have become so completely self-centered are always in conflict with themselves. They are in constant need of counseling from the pastor or a psychiatrist—always requesting some sympathetic soul or prayer group to pray for them. They measure the success or failure of the prayer according to whether their mood is up or down.

Their condition is not improved by non-Christian psychiatry, even though their problem of adjustment suggests many emotional symptoms commonly seen in the natural (unsaved) individual. Psychotherapy, tranquilizers, or even electric shock, may lessen the tension temporarily. Nevertheless, the Christian is still confronted with his soul problem, which can be solved only by "looking unto Jesus the author and finisher of our faith" (Heb. 12:2). Through Christ we overcome Satan and his power over self.

31

Satan's Opportunity

When the Christian fails to walk moment by moment in newness of life, he gives Satan an opportunity to attack the old self. The Christian who has become so self-willed that he does not each moment cast all his cares on the Lord will eventually be overcome by Satan, because the self-will nature endeavors to gather more self-confidence for each conflict. Gradually he depends more and more on self until self has crowded God out. This can imply only one thought, and that is that the self-will is in fellowship with Satan.

When the Christian forgets his position in Christ, he makes self-decisions and goes in the power of the old self-nature. Under these circumstances Satan is able to attack the Christian. Satan energizes and uses the power and intellect of self for his purpose. This, of course, is a subtle, gradual process in which Satan aspires to overcome the spiritual growth by energizing self to become master. When this has been accomplished, the Christian loses his testimony and appears spiritually anemic.

Too often Christians lose this most important battle when they try by force of will to reject unpleasant thoughts. This centers the mind on the problem, making the problem the center of attention instead of Christ. When the problem is paramount in the mind, Christ is set aside. In extreme cases the problem overshadows everything, and the mind cannot turn from the problem to carry on necessary duties of daily routine.

In this dilemma the Christian patient may realize that he should pray and submit (James 4:7) his thoughts to Christ for strength for the battle. But when this hassling with Satan has gone on for a long time, the Christian is spiritually anemic from lack of Bible reading. He feels dejected because he has not been in communion with the Lord. He feels useless because he has lost his testimony. He avoids the fellowship of Christians because he is afraid they will see there is something lacking in his spiritual life. He feels persecuted because his fellow Christians cannot see the sense of all the emotional upheaval. Pityingly he says that they avoid him and don't like him. He even accuses them of not praying for him.

The emotional struggle increases in intensity over a period of time. The symptoms produced and expressed by mental and physical suffering will not be different psychiatrically from symptoms expressed by the unsaved, except that the Christian will occasionally express a desire for fellowship with God, which self has displaced. To the non-Christian psychiatrist these references to God usually suggest a delusional complex from too much Bible reading and religious fellowship.

When the Christian continues to hassle with Satan, the tension eventually produces physical symptoms in various organs of the body, finally causing the organ, gland, skin or muscle to become so energized it becomes ill. Even in the final

33

situation the mind has been so energized by Satan it will not yield, even if the struggle destroys the physical body in death.

In order to grow to spiritual maturity and reach perfection in Christ, the born-again Christian must constantly adjust to the spiritual life he has been planted or born into. He must constantly reckon self dead and buried in Christ. He must be on the alert, keeping in mind the Apostle Peter's warning to the Christian to "be vigilant" lest Satan catch him not casting all of his care on Christ moment by moment.

How Satan Takes Over Self

The Christian whose thoughts are all centered on anxious problems (worry) has been hassling with the problem, thereby enlarging the problems until his mental processes engulf his whole being. His self-nature has been taken over by Satan, but he permitted this. When the Christian does not keep self hidden in Christ, Satan attacks the old self-nature, attempting to beguile the Christian into resorting to the old habit of living in accordance with his self-disposition as he did before he was born again and became a new creature. In fact, this Christian takes on worldly methods of solving his problem because Satan has drawn him back into this world which is Satan's domain.

Eventually, grappling with the problem saps the patient's energy and depresses him. Then he is so completely bound to worry that he is a slave to

Satan. While he continually dotes on his worry, he is in fellowship with Satan and out of fellowship with God.

The patient has not lost his salvation, for he cries out to God and wants to reestablish his fellowship with Him. But self will not let him set worry aside even long enough to read God's Word or to concentrate on the Word when it is preached to him. Satan has frightened him into believing that he might lose his mind if he does not constantly guard his thinking.

When we see a Christian overcome and engulfed with worry, we can only conclude that he has not completely counted on the fact of the crucifixion and burial of self in Christ. Christ is not his life. Self, engulfed in worry, is his tormented life.

It seems the difficulty is in the fact that many newly born Christians do not comprehend the status of being crucified, dead, buried and resurrected in Christ. They do not seem to center their faith, hope and trust in what Christ did for them, nor do they understand that being born again puts them into Christ. Their desires and wills should now center on Christ because they are new creatures in Him.

When your will and your desire are crucified with Christ, there is no self-desire or "I" to wander back to the former life because "Christ liveth in" you (Gal. 2:20).

In fact, the old self, the "I," is not open to attack by Satan to entice us back to his domain when we saturate our thoughts in Christ as our Lord. When we have sweet communion with our Lord, self is overshadowed by our spiritual fellowship with Him.

In Bondage to Self

Christians with emotional problems have permitted their minds to become encumbered with thoughts, feelings and doubts that have their origin in self. This should not happen to the Christian.

The Christian in bondage to self is very difficult to help because his self-centered mind is not open to spiritual teachings. He is constantly on the defensive, saying, "I doubt my salvation. I had no experience when I was saved. I don't have a right feeling. Maybe my mind is so far gone from this worry that I have lost my ability to think. My doctor said my trouble is mental."

When the nervous Christian is convinced that his suffering is in his mind, all his thoughts and concerns are centered on self. He is completely wrapped up in self.

Self-centered Christians, who do not overcome, are blind to the suffering they cause others and see only their own suffering. They do not want to see that their suffering is due to conflict in the soul.

But there is hope for Christians who are willing to see that their suffering is in the soul. As the Christian cries out today, "I don't want to be this way, but I am trapped," the Apostle Paul also confessed, "For what I would, that do I not; but

36

what I hate, that do I" (Rom. 7:15). The way out
of this conflict for the Christian today is the same
as the Apostle Paul found when he cried out: "O
wretched man that I am! who shall deliver me from
the body of this death? I thank God through Jesus
Christ our Lord" (Rom. 7:24,25).

The Battle Is Spiritual

It takes some Christians a long time to awaken
to the fact that they are involved in a spiritual
warfare against Satan, the prince of the power of
the air. The more self-centered seem never to come
to this realization. First, they are not aware that
there is a prince of the power of the air. Second,
their self-centered natures turn to the world with
its diversions and tranquilizers for release from the
fatiguing spiritual battle. Satan has them believing
that they are suffering from some aspects of
nervous breakdown for which they should seek
psychiatric help. This diabolic subterfuge turns
them to the world with their anxieties and fears
instead of seeking fellowship with the Lord.

Spiritual Christians recognize that their warfare
is a spiritual battle and that they are warring
against evil spirits under the rule of the prince of
the power of the air. Spiritual Christians, being
more mature, are conscious of their relationship
with Christ as Lord. Before they let self overpower
them, control them, and put them into bondage to
the evil powers, they cry out to God for
deliverance. They also may struggle against the

37

spirit which attempts to make them believe God has forsaken them. Nevertheless, they have victory through Christ in that they do not wrestle with the evil thoughts and self-problems, but keep their eyes on Christ as Lord and trust in His resurrection power over Satan.

As the Christian desires and yields to the love of God, the old ego, the "I," evaporates with all the facets of self such as self-will, self-love, self-pity and self-righteousness.

There is only one way to defeat self and that is to reckon on the fact that the self has been crucified with Christ.

Chapter 3

Babes in Christ

For an understanding of the background of the babe in Christ, let us compare his spiritual infancy with that of the physical growth of the natural-born baby. Both have been given the instinct to desire nourishment soon after birth.

The natural-born baby is instinctively ready to nurse at the mother's breast soon after birth. In like manner, the babe in Christ desires nourishment, the "sincere milk of the word," immediately after being born into Christ. In both instances God gives the instinct.

By inspiration of the Holy Spirit, Peter gave us special light on this desire of the newborn babe in Christ. We read in I Peter 2:2: "As newborn babes, desire the sincere milk of the word, that ye may grow thereby."

It is apparent from this that the spirit of the newborn babe in Christ desires the unadulterated Word of God. He desires the true gospel and not some adulterated substitute.

The desire of the babe in Christ to know more about God and to grow in the Lord is truly

God-given. It is very plain in the inspired verses of I Peter 2:2,3 that the Holy Spirit causes the babe in Christ to want to grow in Christ through the Word.

The Holy Spirit is trying to teach us in Peter's first epistle that we Christians should lay aside the various carnal traits, "all malice, and all guile, and hypocrisies, and envies, and all evil speakings," that beset us, and consider that as babes in Christ we did not start with a desire for carnality, but with a desire for the "sincere milk of the word" (2:1,2).

Undernourished

As a physician I know that an undernourished baby is an easy prey for any disease that comes along. He also has greater difficulty in throwing off various infections and childhood diseases, which may leave him in a chronic debilitated state. This hinders his proper childhood development and frequently handicaps him for life.

Likewise, in the spiritual sense, one who is newly born again must be properly nourished on the "sincere milk of the word." His spiritual formula must be increased to satisfy his spiritual needs.

Along with the physical handicap of the undernourished baby, there is usually an emotional sequela (nervousness) which sets the stage for an emotional pattern that grows with the child.

The babe in Christ who is not sufficiently nourished at the right time can—and often does—substitute adulterated religious food to satisfy his craving for nourishment. This will not only stifle his spiritual growth, but it will also leave him chronically spiritually debilitated.

Probably the largest percentage of Christians who suffer from emotional problems and from spiritual malnutrition are carnal Christians who were spiritually dwarfed at the babe-in-Christ stage of growth. In other words, they were so handicapped that they could not reach a state of spiritual maturity.

When a Christian suffers from spiritual malnutrition, he is unable to resist the satanic darts of doubt, anxiety and fear which arise from the old self-nature. These cause him to be taken up with Scripture verses which he interprets apart from their context. Thus, he becomes confused over the scriptural distinctions of standing and state as well as law and grace.

Satanic Confusion

When a babe in Christ is undernourished, Satan comes to him as an angel of light and entices him by offering him nourishment that seems palatable and reasonable. Satan does this by appealing to the believer's old nature. Since the believer is still a babe, he can be easily deceived into believing that he is being nourished on the Word of God. "Bloodless" cults—which are Satan's deceivers—often use biblical terminology to make their teachings palatable.

41

Satan confuses the unsuspecting babe who starts out with much zeal but ceases to grow. Spiritual growth stops because he has not had sufficient nourishment from God's Word, and he turns to Satan's substitutes.

In this state it is more difficult to convince him of his heresy than to convince an individual who has never had any Christian teaching. In many cases his satanically inspired zeal will drive him to disseminate his false teaching as biblical truth. He may turn out to be an ardent proselyte for a cult religion and remain spiritually crippled for life.

Spiritual Miscarriage

We can draw another parallel from the physical world—that of miscarriage.

Several years ago one of my patients, after becoming a Christian, desired water baptism. She expressed to her husband that she hoped he would join her in the ordinance. He agreed, without considering the full significance of water baptism from the scriptural standpoint.

Oh, yes, he believed in Jesus and, like many nominal Christians, he was willing to make a commitment to Christ with the mouth. But there was no heart change, evidenced by the fact that there was no blossoming out of radiant joy so characteristically expressed by a new babe in Christ.

Shortly after they were baptized they were invited to a social gathering of their former worldly friends. As was the custom of previous gatherings, alcoholic beverages were served. My patient refused to imbibe and gave a strong testimony in the spirit of love for Christ.

When the drinks were offered to her husband, he made no protest but partook as on previous occasions. Someone in the group chided him, saying, "I thought you were baptized at the same time as your wife." To which he replied, "Yes, I was baptized, but it didn't take."

This is a case of spiritual miscarriage. He heard the Word. He made a verbal commitment to Christ and was baptized, but he stopped short of being made alive—being born again.

He is a type of nominal Christians who sit with us in our Christian fellowship: "Having a form of godliness, but denying the power thereof" (II Tim. 3:5) and "ever learning and never able to come to the knowledge of the truth" (v. 7).

From the Old to the New

Christians should realize that when the babe in Christ is not received into Christian fellowship with a spirit of rejoicing, he has a struggle with the old self and with Satan. The old self-nature with all of its habits, tastes and delights wants to draw him back into his former self-life. Of course, the evil spirits will appeal to his reason, trying to convince him that he is making himself uncomfortable by leaving the old and trying to adapt himself to a

43

new fellowship which he has probably despised in the past.

In fact, Satan may approach the babe in Christ who is in one of those doubtful, despairing moments with a fear that he ought to reconsider his new joy before he goes too far in his new venture and becomes a religious fanatic. Satan may also encourage him to evaluate his mental status in the light of what he has heard and believed about people going insane over religion.

A number of my Christian patients have confessed that for a short time after they were saved, they did not enter wholeheartedly into the Christian fellowship for fear of being considered fanatical and unbalanced, of "going overboard on religion."

Quite a few babes in Christ, who had a true conversion experience, confessed that the changeover after the new birth was a "hard, dry labor" experience. They did not feel comfortable with the old fellowship because they could not give themselves as freely to former pleasures. Therefore, their unsaved friends could not enjoy their fellowship as in previous times; their very presence was a wet blanket to worldly pleasures. Yet, as one Christian said, "I did not seem to belong to the Christian group as I had nothing to contribute. I did not know the Bible as well as they did."

Disillusionment

There is still another condition the newly born-again babe in Christ must often face.

44

Unreasonable as it is, Christians who are long on religious and moral conduct, but lacking in Christian charity, are intolerant with the babe in Christ who does not blossom forth as a mature Christian in a few days after salvation. This pharisaical attitude creates a problem for new Christians who, not grounded in the Word, may imitate the manner of walk of the worldly Christian. They will look upon Jesus as a social teacher, rather than learning to "know him, and the power of his resurrection, and the fellowship of his sufferings" (Phil. 3:10).

Satan thus deceives these new Christians and puts them into bondage to a false conception of Christianity. He binds them so completely that it is virtually impossible for them to be enlightened to their state of Christianity.

Too often we Christians fail the babe in Christ because we assume he can take care of himself, forgetting it took us a long time to learn how to rightly divide the Word of Truth.

There is another disillusioning experience to which new Christians are often subjected by older Christians (not necessarily mature). New Christians are given responsibilities in the Christian fellowship before they have had an opportunity to feed on the milk of the Word and to grow spiritually.

One novice said, "The very first church business meeting we had after I was baptized and taken into the church, they elected me treasurer. I was pleased with their confidence in me. I soon found out why I was elevated to that position so

45

soon. It was the treasurer's job to go around and collect the church pledges when they were due. I found out no one cared for the task because some did not want to pay up. They did not act as I thought Christians should act. They acted unfriendly to me. It was not my fault; I had to ask them when they were negligent in their pledges."

This babe in Christ came into the church without any or much spiritual instruction. Instead of being nurtured in the Spirit, works were emphasized. Needless to say, his disillusionment caused him to leave the church and turn to religious so-called arms of the church.

A young lady said, "I was given a Sunday school class to teach. I was surprised they would ask me. I was of the opinion a Sunday school class teacher did not smoke or go to shows and dances. I figured they knew that part of my life, so I concluded I must be all right or they would not have asked me. I thought they figured I was saved. At least, their asking me gave me that assurance. I never felt too confident about my conduct until years later at a revival meeting when I repented and gave my heart to the Lord."

Spiritual Immaturity

Not all babes in Christ grow up to the same spiritual maturity, just as we have babies who do not grow up to the same physical maturity. We physicians try to determine what hinders the physical body of the baby from developing properly; likewise, Christians want to know what hinders the spiritual babe from growing up.

We cannot blame "the sincere milk of the word." He has tasted it and had joy in it, but something happened to take away the desire for "the sincere milk of the word."

Perhaps he has not confessed and forsaken all the desires of his former life of sin. Self has not been counted as crucified. He is aware and conscious of "the sincere milk of the word"—that it is good; but self comes up as a temptation. He begins to find excuses for not feeding on the Word with as much delight as when he first became a Christian.

He says that he can't find time to read and meditate because of his busy schedule, or he says that he can't understand all of what he reads. And lastly, of course, it condemns him for the pleasure he gets out of worldly things. So he gives less and less time to the Word of God and more place to the things of self.

The babe in Christ who had such a hopeful beginning now comes into bondage of self-desires. He loses his craving for the "sincere milk of the word," and he has lost the initial radiant joy that makes a spiritual babe so appealing. He now strives to do commendable works so that he will have a rightful place in the Christian fellowship.

Such a Christian is not thoroughly prepared for the obstacles with which he will be confronted. As the baby's formula must be increased according to his need, and as the natural body requires increased

47

rations for sustenance and growth as the physical being develops, so it is also essential that the spiritual man partake more and more of the divinely provided food, the Word of God, that he may grow to spiritual maturity. When he neglects to nourish his spiritual being, he gives Satan a foothold in tempting him to follow carnal desires.

It is the carnal desires and concerns of Christians that create emotional conflicts and so-called nervous breakdowns.

Spiritual Rest

The first thing God claims for His new Christians is rest: "Come unto me, all ye that labour and are heavy laden, and I will give you rest" (Matt. 11:28).

Too often we urge new Christians to get busy in some church activity instead of teaching them to feed on the "sincere milk of the word" that they may grow thereby. God wants them to grow in spirit so that the works will be Spirit-inspired, rather than being generated by the self-nature.

It is apparent the new life in Christ gives the new Christian a desire to grow in Christ, for he is open, eager and, in a sense, inspired by his new nature to serve in things of the Lord.

Thus, the new babe in Christ, because of his eagerness to be obedient and grow in spiritual matters, can become confused because he cannot discern what is best and proper for his growth.

48

Frequently he accepts any and all church assignments given to him by the brethren. This finally results in his doing many works, but his soul is left barren because of his lack of time in feeding on "the sincere milk of the word" so that he might grow to spiritual maturity.

Eventually he boggs down with his works and becomes tired and frustrated because he has not acquired spiritual grace to deal with spiritual problems.

A rather lengthy personal history of a patient, including his physical and emotional symptoms, will give the reader a clearer picture of what happens to a babe in Christ when he does not take time for his "rest periods" in the Lord and when he neglects to take proper nourishment for his soul.

The History

The patient was not a Christian and had not been reared in a Christian home. He consulted me because he was suffering from an anxiety state that had gone so far as to produce psychosomatic symptoms, which made him introspective. He imagined that various sensations and pains in his body could increase to such a state as to cause his death. Therefore, he was constantly seeking medical relief but without any success. He could not be cured of his somatic symptoms as long as his anxiety, fears and tensions continued to aggravate the symptoms.

49

On the other hand, the anxiety state and fears—which started in childhood—grew with him as he grew to manhood, causing the tension to be expressed in various organs of his body, which he feared would become afflicted.

The anxiety about his physical condition made him so anxious that he had a constant awareness of the symptoms, or functioning of various organs of his body. He started out with gastritis, which was followed by other symptoms: colitis, muscular spasms suggesting paralysis, and many bizarre sensations in his chest which constantly made him have a fear of being a heart patient.

His suffering—that is, his worry, anxiety and fear of going insane—reached such a state that his thoughts were completely taken up with himself. He could not concentrate on his work and make a livelihood for himself and his family.

When he consulted me, he was afraid of losing his mind because he could not concentrate on anything but his thoughts, which went from worry to worry. He had been warned by other physicians that if he did not do something soon he would have a nervous breakdown. Therefore, he wondered if he had not already done so much damage to his brain that he could not be helped.

Of course, his initial interview was a long drawn-out recitation of his many fears, trying to get assurance that he was not so far gone that he was hopeless. While enumerating all the things he did to get relief, he rather glibly said, "I even prayed about it."

I took this last statement as an open door to inquire into his spiritual condition. To many who are still groping in darkness, "I prayed about it" is an idiom denoting their utter helplessness in a situation, yet implying that they have an inherent awareness of a godhead, as depicted in Romans 1:19,20.

I laid the Bible in his lap and had him read directly from God's Word the verses I designated. Having him read from the Bible proved to him that the words were not the psychiatrist's words used just for encouragement. They were from God's Word. Through experience, I have found that having the patient read the holy words from the Bible has a profound spiritual power. The patient's mind then seems open to follow the biblical explanation regarding his spiritual condition—that "all have sinned and come short of the glory of God" (Rom. 3:23); that he needs to repent and turn from the world with its lust.

It is essential that the patient grasp the full significance of the fact that Christ made an atonement for his sins on the cross of Calvary.

When the Holy Spirit spoke to this patient's heart, he acknowledged that he was a lost sinner. He was eager to hear and tried to comprehend what Christ did for him on the cross of Calvary. He asked many questions about the forgiveness of sins and had a strong sense of guilt regarding his past sins. He confessed his sins to God. He humbled himself to ask his wife for forgiveness of his past unfaithfulness and lack of consideration. He asked

51

God to take away his desire for liquor, gambling, lying, tobacco and cheating.

There was a genuine repentance and a turning from former worldly lusts, not just an attitude of believing and a commitment to Christ because of a head knowledge. It was a genuine confession from a regenerated heart.

There was a visible transformation. He wanted to discuss questions about the Bible and his attitude regarding his walk and worldly conduct. The apprehension of bodily sensations became less intense.

His joy was so overflowing that he caused his wife to want to partake of his joy. His wife and child were both saved as a result of his exemplifying life and testimony. The family found joy in reading the Bible and listening to gospel broadcasts.

Later, this patient's wife told me: "It was good that my husband had to become a psychiatric patient and go to you for help, else I would never have been saved. I thought I was saved and was all taken up in a modernistic church. I did not know any better. I thought that was Christianity until my husband was saved and I saw such a completely changed man.

"He explained to me what you told him about what Christ did on the cross of Calvary—how He shed His blood to wash away our sins. I could believe this because I saw what happened to my husband. He was a changed man and was so different to me. He had me read the verses you

52

pointed out in the Bible. They really had meaning to me now. So I can say somewhat like the psalmist, 'It was good that my husband was afflicted, that I might be saved.' Otherwise we never would have been saved.''

After this patient had tasted, he found that the Lord was gracious to him. He enjoyed His fellowship and was released from much of his anxiety. This was in proportion to the faith he was able to establish in Christ. He quit smoking, drinking, using profane language, and he desired fellowship with Christians.

His business required that he attend stockholders' dinner meetings where they all drank liquor. He attended the meetings but refused the liquor. This brought ridicule and laughter at first, but eventually it became an established custom at stockholders' meetings to find a glass of soft drink by his plate.

Almost immediately after his conversion he attempted to read the Bible with his family, although his wife took the lead. He took his family to a church where his spirit was fed with the true gospel. Even as a babe, he at once sensed the difference between the life-giving gospel and the social, "bloodless" preaching of the modernistic churches.

The patient now made a habit of listening regularly to Christian radio broadcasts. If his former friends intruded on this special time, he would persist in listening to the program. Eventually they learned not to visit him during his

53

radio devotional hours. It became evident to them that he thought so much of some gospel broadcasts that he would not miss them for anybody. Tithing to the Lord and giving love offerings to his church and to Christian radio work became a habit with him even as a babe in Christ.

This patient's psychosomatic symptoms lessened greatly in intensity as he turned his thoughts to the Lord. No longer was he fearful that when his heart palpitated it would go out of control and cause him to have a fatal heart attack or a stroke. He was able to refrain from constantly feeling and counting his pulse when he faced a tense situation, wondering how his heart was performing under stress.

What May Happen to the Babe in Christ

This babe in Christ, like thousands of others, started out with zeal. He was desiring the milk of the Word and was growing thereby. But alas! Gradually and insidiously Satan's emissaries attacked him through his pride of life. He became so taken up with his business and the desire to impress his superiors that he cut short his Bible reading and curtailed his listening to gospel broadcasts.

Simultaneously his anxiety symptoms began to increase. He became more introspective about his bodily sensations, asking himself, Is this sensation a sign of something I had better see the doctor about? Is this pain in my left shoulder a sign of an impending heart attack?

Especially would the symptoms be pronounced if he heard about the death of a friend. Invariably he would question the relatives of the deceased about the symptoms that had caused the death. Then he would be haunted by those symptoms.

Periodically he would have a resurgence of Bible reading, especially when his family took the lead. He experienced for himself that Bible reading was not just a mental diversion, for he received spiritual power from God when he would keep his eyes on Christ and meditate on spiritual things. But his self-nature had been so reactivated by self-indulgence that it was difficult for him to forsake the worldly things for God.

He worked long hours, even into the night on many occasions. His wife encouraged him to get his rest and even brought his breakfast to him on a tray. While sitting up in bed to eat his breakfast he watched TV.

When questioned as to why he did not use this time to read his Bible or have his wife read to him, he frequently alibied by saying that he did not care to read; that he left the Bible reading to his wife. Or he would retort, "I need some time for recreation. I need to know what is going on in the world."

He took his family to Sunday school and church, but he remained in the car during Sunday school because he was afraid he would reveal his ignorance of the Bible. He feared they might call

55

on him for an opinion, and others might not think much of his opinion.

When it was voted to paint the church building, he volunteered to donate all the paint. When the church was remodeled on the outside, he paid for the materials—even though it was a real financial burden.

He fretted over the fact that they accepted his money but never put him on the church board. He said, "I thought the pastor could have seen to that; in fact, we were so close that I had him over for dinner on the average of once every two weeks, and I thought he liked me."

He was never at ease in church because he was afraid they might call on him to pray. He had requested that the pastor and the superintendent of the Sunday school refrain from calling on him; yet he was afraid they might forget and embarrass him.

It embarrassed him that his wife and daughter testified in public. He objected to his wife's singing solos and in duets, fearing she might "go flat."

He was always quick to detect any lack of Christian charity in others, but he refused to be enlightened to the fact that he no longer had a desire for spiritual things.

His thoughts now were no longer on Christ and what He had done for him on the cross of Calvary, but on what he could do in his self-efforts. These became his code of religious living. He wanted to be praised for his religious works and moral conduct.

To Spiritual Maturity

The following brief history of a patient who became born again during treatment is a beautiful picture of what happens when self and its desires have been crucified.

The anxiety state of this patient, who was suffering from an emotional problem, was based on a guilt that started in his youth. Finally, it caused him to have psychosomatic symptoms.

He would awaken in the morning with an urgent, profuse diarrhea, which lessened in degree as the day progressed and his mind was occupied with duties of the day. Occasionally, during the day when his environmental situation triggered the urgency, he would have spasms in the lower bowel. Medication was unsuccessful in his case because the medication could not change his thinking, which brought on the sudden urges in his lower bowel.

Psychiatry was not new to this patient. He had been given electric shock and insulin shock. Also, he had run the gamut of each new tranquilizer as soon as it was put on the pharmaceutical shelf as a cure for tension.

All of these experiences made him dubious of psychiatry ever relieving him of his affliction. Yet he could not stop; something had to be done. He was even more skeptical of the virtue of psychiatry because he was convinced that some of the therapy had worsened his condition and had left him more anxious than when he had first placed his condition in the hands of psychiatry.

As a last resort, he sought help from a religious counselor. However, the counselor was unable to cope with the medical phase of diarrhea. Therefore, the counselor suggested he turn again to psychiatry, which could deal with the somatic symptoms while psychotherapy was being instituted for the cause of the emotional problem.

When this patient came to me for treatment he was an unregenerate man, trying to find solace in some Bible verses that had been given to him to divert his mind from his worry. They had no more effect than quoting a beautiful stanza of poetry. The Bible verses were without power to him because his natural mind could not comprehend their spiritual implications.

No doubt the Holy Spirit had this man marked for salvation because of his willingness to admit he had no strength in himself to overcome his emotional problem. He was now groping in the religious realm, but he could not find the "Way."

God's plan of salvation was explained to him by having him read the appropriate Bible passages directly from the Bible. As mentioned previously, this does away with much doubt and the idea that it could only be psychological reasoning.

As the patient read the Word he came to a realization of his need of Christ, repented of his sins, and received Jesus Christ as his Saviour.

As a babe in Christ he radiated joy and was keenly interested in knowing more about God's Word. This annoyed his wife, who was certain "a person need not go overboard on religion."

She attributed his "religious zeal" to the fact that he must have fallen into the hands of the wrong psychiatrist, believing that the psychiatrist was a religious fanatic. Because his wife did not like his change of appetite from worldly things to a spiritual life, he met considerable opposition to his psychiatric treatment for his anxiety neurosis.

He performed his professional duties as formerly, but with more sincerity and honesty. He took a keen interest in his church and started to teach an adult Bible class, which grew until it comprised most of the adults in the church.

He had a desire for "the sincere milk of the word." He not only studied his Bible carefully, but he also read the biographies of the spiritual giants of the past century. He wanted to find out what they did to grow to spiritual maturity. For instance, he read some of Dr. H. A. Ironside's books. He found that Dr. Ironside got much of his spiritual inspiration from the writings of C. H. Mackintosh. Naturally, he acquired everything that came from the pen of Mackintosh. In fact, the spiritual growth of this patient motivated me to acquire and study these writings also.

This patient spent much time in Christian bookstores, searching for sound scriptural interpretations of the doctrines of the Word. He now came to the psychiatric sessions, not to discuss the Freudian theories of anxiety, but to analyze the Bible. Thus he learned to put his trust in Christ and have Christ as his goal for thinking.

After awhile there was really not much desire to discuss psychiatric reasons for man's actions. As a regenerated man he no longer saw his problems through the world's eyes, but he viewed everything from his relationship to Christ.

At no time in his babe-in-Christ stage of growth did he seem to have a pull back to the uncrucified self. He knew by experience that whenever there was such a battle, self must be reckoned crucified, dead and buried with Christ. By this constant going back to assure himself of his relationship with Christ and keeping his eyes on Him, he had the resurrection power.

Whenever Satan tried to reactivate some self-trait, my patient learned by repeated testings that he must not let the imaginations of former self grow in his heart until it became a desire to want fulfillment or release. He learned how to cast his thinking on Christ and to bring into captivity every thought to the obedience of Christ (II Cor. 10:5).

During one consultation the patient gave this testimony: "In a careless or off moment I ask myself, Will this trouble ever come back to haunt me again? Will I ever get as low as I have been before? What really became of my anxiety?

"I can recall it and when something makes me a little tense, my thoughts go back to my diarrhea symptoms. Occasionally I sit down and think this over and wonder how I worked this out step by step in order that if it ever came back I would know what to do to cure myself. Then I suddenly realize, as I reckon that I am in Christ and He is in me, that nothing can happen to me because the self has been crucified with Christ, and the self is not free to get tense anymore."

This patient was emancipated by keeping his thoughts on Christ and what He did for him on the cross of Calvary.

Chapter 4

Yet Carnal

When we Christians do not reckon on the crucifixion and burial of self with Christ, we are "yet carnal" (I Cor. 3:3). This carnal nature continues to remain as a thorn in the flesh of the Christian to harass his fellowship with Christ.

Christians who are "yet carnal" do not seem to realize that the self which has not been reckoned crucified strives against the Spirit of God. This striving creates worry, fear, anxiety, bodily tensions, and a myriad of psychosomatic symptoms—so-called nervous symptoms.

These nervous Christians, because they are more carnal than spiritual, live and move about in a "yet carnal" atmosphere. They reason and think carnally. Being energized by their carnal disposition, they look to the world for an answer to their problems.

Christians with emotional problems often are at the root of the dissension in many of our church and Christian fellowship groups. They have a driving zeal for doing works in the church. They aspire to hold positions of authority in the church.

62

These frustrated individuals may become so disturbed over their inability to accomplish good works of their self-nature that they create tensions and divisions in the body of believers. When one member of the Body of Christ suffers, all members suffer (I Cor. 12:26).

The dissenter, driven by his carnal nature, creates dissension and schism among the believers. Some will be with him in his zeal; others will be against him. The Apostle Paul asked, "For whereas there is among you envying, and strife, and divisions, are ye not carnal?" (I Cor. 3:3).

A dissenter among believers is not only a problem to the local church, but he finally becomes a problem to himself. Invariably he projects his frustrations and anger onto the spiritual leaders in the church, claiming they are against him. He does not see that he is the problem, but convinces himself that the spiritual leaders are to blame for his unhappiness and emotional state.

Satan generally drives such a carnal Christian to vindicate himself until he becomes so upset that he requires counseling. In a spirit of vindictiveness, he naturally seeks someone to confirm his attitude. First, he will consult a pastor or member of another church, anticipating confirmation. The real need is for him to be taken into the Word so he will see his need for the milk of the Word.

If he does not grow spiritually, his frustrations will eventually produce psychosomatic symptoms;

63

that is, organic symptoms such as stomach ulcers, mucous colitis, indigestion, hypertension and many others—all organized by some nervous tension, not by a physical disease.

Should he continue to live in his carnality, he may become so emotionally upset he will need psychiatric help. Under the guidance of non-Christian psychiatry, usually he will be encouraged to avoid the problem that frustrates him. This would be to avoid the fellowship of Christians. Probably this same individual would have no problem of adjusting in a civic club.

The verbal testimony of many Christians is often not very convincing; neither do they by their fruits and manner of life inspire the unsaved to become Christians. Too many are satisfied with salvation only, and they do not care to mature to discipleship. They may acknowledge Jesus as Saviour, but they refuse to make Him the Lord of their lives.

The Bible calls these Christians "carnal" because they have not reckoned their flesh nature as having been crucified with Christ. They still love the old self more than they love Christ who bought them. They are aware of their attitude, and they resent being classified as "carnal Christians." Neither do these Christians like to be called "babes in Christ," even though they have failed to add one inch to their spiritual growth. Of course, they are not really babes, because they have no desire for the sincere milk of the word" (I Pet. 2:2).

The Apostle Paul wrote that the Christians in the Corinthian church had not grown sufficiently to be taken off milk. Then in I Corinthians 3:3, Paul, under the direction of the Holy Spirit, enumerated some symptoms of carnality: "For ye are yet carnal: for whereas there is among you envying, and strife, and divisions, are ye not carnal, and walk as men?"

Today we have the identical carnality symptoms, but many evangelists and pastors are careful not to offend Christians by labeling them as "carnal Christians." One evangelist, in all seriousness, suggested that I not use the word "carnal" in my writings, but rather use some psychiatric nomenclature such as: immature, maladjusted, nervous, sick, worldly, emotional.

Truly it is a sign of the perilous times to refrain from labeling people who are lovers of themselves as "carnal" and to use some psychiatric terminology that would excuse the sin in the heart as an "emotional illness" of the mind.

Carnal Christian patients want to believe that their carnal state is a mental condition. They then can feel justified to treat their problem as a psychiatric problem rather than a carnal condition of the heart which marks it as sin. This may explain why so many carnal Christians prefer to have their emotional problems dealt with by non-Christian psychiatrists rather than by Christian counselors. The former turn to the world and away from Christ; whereas the latter turn to Christ and away from the world.

Wanting Attention

After leaving the hospital a patient said, "Since I got out of the hospital they pay so little attention to me. While in the hospital I received attention and it made me feel important. Now I guess I am mad at them for neglecting me. I feel so antagonistic and inferior around people."

A middle-aged lady is cited here as another example of this type of problem. Whenever she appealed to her Christian friends for sympathy and understanding, they invariably turned her to God's Word in order to get her mind off self. Her usual response came in these words: "I am just a babe in Christ. You must not expect as much from me as you might from others. I was just saved three years ago."

Now why does this three-year-old Christian insist on calling herself a babe? A natural-born, normal, three-year-old child does not want to be called a baby. The patient does not want to grow up spiritually. She is afraid of criticism of her way of life. She has become a feeding problem. She is allergic to the milk of the Word. Somewhere in the past she has been conditioned against the authority of the Bible. She does not want to grow to spiritual maturity lest she might have to leave her self-reasonings, which she loves more than she loves Christ.

She has refused to eat what is considered proper food for a babe in Christ. She is stunted, irritable and intolerable because she indulges in food that is not good for her—that cannot give her spiritual stamina. She is antagonistic to any effort to get her to take wholesome nourishment to overcome the debilitating anemia which leaves her mind and spirit open to all kinds of counterfeit religions.

She concludes that she is nervous and needs release from her situation. Because she does not want to change, she goes from church to church until she finds a fellowship that will not disturb her way of life. She has the attitude of the mixed multitude that came up out of Egypt with the Israelites. She wants to enjoy the blessings of Christian fellowship but does not want to live as a Christian should.

In retrospect, one patient made this observation about his Christian growth: "While I attended a liberal church I saw little or no mental confusion. I see why; there was no separation. It was so worldly.

"When I joined a fundamental church I had a hard time adjusting. I knew they were right, but I had an inner resentment against those who lived morally upright. I was against the pastor and the Sunday school teachers. I hunted out people who had the same feeling I had. I started a little clique. I was always laying for the Sunday school class teacher. I would needle him about some principle on which we differed when I felt I had one or two on my side. I resented him because he was successful; I wanted to be able to teach as well as

67

he could. In fact, I thought they should ordain me as a lay preacher."

Another patient said, "I always resented people who were successful. I suffered all my life from inferiority. I want to do something to have people notice me. I try to do it by tearing people down to my size. I started a hate clique in the church. I had the Sunday school superintendent on my side. We nearly always had Sunday dinner together and we always had 'roast preacher.'

"Three years ago I developed heart pains in my chest. Doctors cannot find anything organically wrong. It is all in my mind. It gets worse when I get frightened; even scary things on TV bring on the pains. I know the Lord is dealing with me. I am better since I am getting into the Word. I changed my attitude. I dropped the clique. The pastor and I get along fine."

Don't Want to Be Different

The problem with many carnal Christians is that they do not want to be different from the world. For instance, we often hear the self-assuring expression, "Yes, I joined the church, but I did not go overboard like some do." There is a hesitation to grow up and be useful for the Lord. They are afraid they might be considered maladjusted by the world.

Christians must be maladjusted to the world. We cannot be adjusted to Christ and be adjusted to the world at the same time. It never works for the

Christians. Matthew 6:24 says, "No man can serve two masters: for either he will hate the one, and love the other; or else he will hold to the one, and despise the other. Ye cannot serve God and mammon."

Carnal Christians desire to be well thought of by the world. They do not want to separate from the world. Instead, they want to take the world with them into the church fellowship. They want Christ to be their Saviour, but not their Lord.

Since they have tasted little, if any, real spiritual fellowship, they remain worldly minded. Because of their spiritual ignorance, Satan uses them as dupes to poke fun at the spiritual Christians, calling them "religious fanatics."

A certain minister who delighted to associate himself with many religious and modernistic social welfare organizations, boasted to some Christians: "These fellowships do not affect my standing with the Christians because the Christians all know where I stand."

However, Christians do not know where he stands. The Bible says, "No man can serve two masters" (Matt. 6:24). We also read: "Wherefore come out from among them, and be ye separate, saith the Lord, and touch not the unclean thing" (II Cor. 6:17).

This minister was not at peace in his spirit, or he would not have deemed it necessary to defend his carnal stand.

No Desire to Give Up Carnality

Every pastor is called upon at times to counsel Christians who come for confirmation of their ways of life rather than to obtain information on how to change them. They want salvation only as an escape guarantee against going to hell; therefore, they retain their worldly philosophy. They do not want to live for the Lord who bought them; they want their own desires. They have a desire to satisfy "the lust of the flesh, and the lust of the eyes, and the pride of life" (I John 2:16).

Strange as it may seem, these Christians insist on living this manner of life in our Christian organizations.

The following excerpts from case histories should awaken God's people to guard the positions of responsibility in our Christian assemblies.

"I can't give up smoking. I feel guilty, but not guilty enough to quit it. To justify myself I look around and say to myself, 'This man smokes and that member of our church smokes.' I lost my interest in the church. I can't enjoy my Bible anymore. I don't read my Bible as much as I read other Christian literature.

"I grew up in a modern church where most everybody smoked. Those who did not smoke were so few that the church would not make an issue of it. In our church the pastor preaches holiness and a separated life. I am not ready to yield.

"I taught a Sunday school class for two years. I smoked and drank whiskey all the while. They

70

would not let me have a class after they found I smoked. I had an unkind feeling toward the pastor."

The above confession was brought out when the patient appealed to me for psychiatric help for an immoral problem involving himself, his wife, and other men. This man confessed that he knew he was rebelling against God, but he did not want to give up the desires of the flesh. He was contented to be carnal.

It is not unusual to hear this type of Christian reason thus about his rebellious attitude: "I guess I criticize and condemn the least little fault in other Christians so I will not be so conscious of my own weakness."

Another patient summed up this attitude in one brief statement: "I try to cut them down to my size."

A young minister, out of the service of the Lord, analyzed himself according to Romans 2:1: "For wherein thou judgest another, thou condemnest thyself; for thou that judgest doest the same things." He said, "Doctor, that really strikes me hard. I see certain hypocrisies in other Christians. I used to fairly gloat over the fact that others had faults. When I make an honest analysis of it, I find I am guilty of that same type of hypocrisy. Can you see why? In the past I subconsciously, or maybe consciously, wanted to find others guilty of the same thing I am."

Satan took advantage of a facet of carnality of this Christian's old nature, the self, that had not

71

been reckoned crucified with Christ. Did the Christian forget this hidden sin? Why did he not confess and repent of it? Why did he keep it in his heart and mind? Because Satan kept this man bound to his carnality.

A certain Christian in the hands of the law on a charge of immorality came seeking help. He was sorry for having been caught, but not sorry for his sin. We had prayer in my office and, at the close of his prayer, I asked why he did not ask God to create in him a clean heart and take out this sin which caused his trouble. To this he sheepishly replied: "I might want to do it again."

Fulfilling the Evil Imaginations of the Heart

Christians are shocked and puzzled when they find certain Christian leaders in their midst who are seemingly zealous about Christian work, but who are in fellowship with Satan. These Christians may appear as angels of light; therefore, on occasion, they deceive the entire Christian fellowship by their works or organizational leadership.

In his own words, let one of my patients give the reason for such zeal: "I see now why I was so active in our organization [a well-known, so-called arm of the church]. I was a hypocrite. The deeper I got into sin, the more energy I exerted in my religious work."

This patient had become involved in homosexuality, in which he indulged for a number of years. He recalled that he gave up family

72

devotions very soon after he yielded to this sin. He made the excuse that he could not find an appropriate time with his family. However, in psychotherapy he said, "I just could not pray anymore in my wife's presence."

In regard to his religious activities, he said, "The more active I was in our organization, and the harder I worked, the less guilt I felt.

"I always felt inferior around other people, especially the leaders in our church; but I wanted to be a leader. So I determined to make a place for myself in some other Christian organization. I was soon elected chairman of the executive committee, and I took pride in the fact that the organization looked up to me for leadership. I was really chesty.

"I was not worshiping God; I was pushing my ego. I did not realize I had so much pride until some members of the organization heard that I had been picked up, and the committee belittled me by requesting my resignation. I can't get over being let down. I can't see why they don't let me hold my office. I was a pillar in the organization and the push behind every project.

"I am discouraged. I don't care to go to the meetings anymore. They just look at me as though I am the black sheep in the herd. I just can't take it. I want what I want!

"When I got caught I was mad at God for not protecting me. Why did He let me get caught? Why didn't He stop me before I brought this disgrace on myself and my family? What about them now?

"I thought as long as I was promoting God's work, and it was progressing, He surely must be with me. I thought when God blesses a work He must be approving it."

In a later interview, the patient said, "I have conquered my sex perversion, but it still runs in my mind. If I just had not made contact with that last guy!"

This patient was really in torment because he did not want to give up his carnality—the lust of the flesh and the pride of life. He was struggling against the pricks of his conscience because he knew he was living in sin.

When the patient came to a better understanding of himself and his spiritual condition, he said, "Really, Doctor, if this had not happened to me when it did, there is no telling what would have happened to me. I can look back and see it all plainly now.

"I was driving myself. I was restless. I was taking some of those new nerve pills. I was heading for a nervous breakdown. At times I wanted to quit. I knew I was wrong, yet my sinful desire was running wild in my mind all the time, except when I was pushing my activities in the organization."

There are three major points in the foregoing history that my records show are more or less characteristic of carnal Christians who do not want to give up their carnality.

First, they usually resolve to reform, or at least to control themselves, lest they repeat the sin and have to suffer humiliating consequences. Notice this patient said, "I have conquered my sex perversion, but it still runs in my mind."

He was confessing at this point that he still had the desire in his heart, but he was endeavoring in his mind to control his heart's desire. He was sorry for having been caught, but there was no repentance with godly sorrow. By his own will he resolved to keep himself from indulging.

The question with these resolutions is, How long will self-will control the deceit in the heart? Jeremiah 17:9 says, "The heart is deceitful above all things, and desperately wicked: who can know it?"

"It still runs in my mind" was a confession that he was still giving place in his heart to sex perversion imaginations. He did not cast down the imaginations (II Cor. 10:5).

Second, he was bitter and angry with God for permitting him to be exposed. His activities for his organization meant much to his weak, self-centered ego. His deceitful heart reasoned that the righteousness of the righteous would deliver him in the day of his transgression. However, God said, "The righteousness of the righteous shall not deliver him in the day of his transgression . . . neither shall the righteous be able to live for his righteousness in the day that he sinneth" (Ezek. 33:12).

This patient was like the mixed multitude that came up out of Egypt with the Israelites. They wanted to share in the blessings of God's people, but they did not want to be obedient to God.

Carnal Christians want Christ as Saviour, but not as Lord.

Third, he became bold in his sin because he was not being punished by God. This bears out the truth of Ecclesiastes 8:11: "Because sentence against an evil work is not executed speedily, therefore the heart of the sons of men is fully set in them to do evil."

This patient was elevated to the highest position of responsibility in the organization by his self-works, not by the power of the Holy Spirit. Carnal Christians do not distinguish between Christian work and religious works. Christian service is inspired by the Holy Spirit; religious works are incited by self.

A Mental Problem or a Spiritual Problem?

When a Christian permits himself to be overwhelmed by the lust in his heart and commits acts of moral degradation, the members of the Christian fellowship are stunned. At such a time, the believers say to each other, "How could a Christian so active in our fellowship commit such a crime?" (It should be called sin.) "How could he commit such an outrage before his Lord?"

Christians will reason that surely he was mentally sick—"No man in his right mind would do such things!"

No, he is not mentally sick. This type of Christian, in the calm of my office away from public pressure, pours out the imaginations of his heart which have been going on for many months and years. Yet he keeps assuring me that during that time he was mentally capable of carrying on his secular work.

From the non-Christian psychiatric viewpoint it is easy to understand why the natural, unregenerate man looks upon acts of sexual misconduct as a mental problem. The natural man is taught to control his passions and evil imaginations by willpower. If and when he is apprehended by the law, he is ashamed that his abnormal conduct is known to society. In self-defense he feigns mental blackout or a lapse of memory.

Christians are also prone to imitate the psychology of the world instead of looking into the Word of God. When they are shocked at the conduct of a fellow Christian, they, too, want to excuse his misconduct—his sin—as a mental sickness, a mental blackout or a lapse of memory. They forget what God has said about such matters through the words of the Apostle James: "But every man is tempted, when he is drawn away of his own lust, and enticed. Then when lust hath conceived, it bringeth forth sin" (1:14,15).

The heart is deceitful, and these imaginations are conceived in the heart. Instead of casting down the imaginations (II Cor. 10:5), men feed on them until the desire to fulfill them becomes so strong that ways and means are devised to fulfill them.

Assaulting the brain with various forms of shock therapy, tranquilizers, LSD, hypnosis, and

77

pummeling the mind with diverting thoughts cannot keep the deceitful heart, full of evil imaginations, from knocking at the mind's door for attention.

The sin, according to the Bible, is in the heart of man, not in the brain.

Chapter 5
Feelings

Many Christians with emotional problems suffer because they do not "feel" saved. A patient opened the interview with the statement: "I know God has forgiven me, but I cannot feel forgiven."

One patient said, "I have not had any special spiritual experience in my life such as a vision or being converted at a revival. I do not have a satisfactory feeling about my salvation."

Another patient said, "I have periods of depression with anguish. I have gone to the altar time and time again in the past eight years but without relief."

A patient who feared she had lost her salvation said, "I had a blessed experience when saved. However, the blessing slipped away because I did not know how to walk spiritually—I didn't read my Bible and pray regularly. Now I cannot get that feeling back. Am I lost?"

A patient who feared God had forsaken her said, "I doubt my salvation because I have no feelings to prove it. I started on my feelings for salvation and now I depend on my feelings. Since I

79

cannot feel forgiven, has God forsaken me because of some past sin?"

Feelings have absolutely nothing to do with our salvation or forgiveness of past sins. We know we are saved because of God's promises, which cannot be broken. The Bible tells us, "Believe on the Lord Jesus Christ, and thou shalt be saved" (Acts 16:31).

The Word of God does not promise that we will "feel" as if we are saved. Instead, it states the simple fact that we are saved when we fulfill God's condition: "That whosoever believeth in him [God's only begotten Son] should not perish, but have everlasting life" (John 3:16).

When we repent of our sins, confess them to God and turn from them, we have the promise of God's forgiveness: "If we confess our sins, he is faithful and just to forgive us our sins, and to cleanse us from all unrighteousness" (I John 1:9).

God's promises have nothing to do with our feelings. When God forgives us He is satisfied about our forgiven sins. Therefore, we should be satisfied and not doubt by looking for a sign, in this case a "feeling." Faith is opposite of feeling. "Faith is . . . the evidence of things not seen" (Heb. 11:1). It is the evidence of things not felt.

Lacking in Faith

Christians repeatedly ask, "How can I get more faith? How can I get faith strong enough to stop doubting my salvation?"

Let us consider first how we get faith in anything. For instance, the worldly man acquires faith by studying all about the subject by which he desires to strengthen his faith. The Christian needs to strengthen his faith in God, and his source of information about spiritual things is God's Word. The Bible says, "Faith cometh by hearing, and hearing by the word of God" (Rom. 10:17). It is the Word of God that gives us the faith.

Our faith grows as we nurture it on the sincere milk of the Word. We increase our faith by feasting on God's Word.

What causes so many of my nervous Christian patients to lack faith in God and to put their confidence in something else? The explanation is simple. They have neglected to feed on the Word which strengthens faith.

Christians who base their faith on feelings are substituting feeling for faith. It should be faith in God that controls the soul, but too often it is feelings of the flesh that control it.

Since feelings are constantly fluctuating, these nervous Christians are unsure of themselves. They run here and there trying to recoup a feeling they once enjoyed. When caught in the clutches of a mood, they become restless and fearful, agitating for a "good" feeling.

Satan Makes Neurotics

Satan's subtlety snatches away faith in God, replacing it with feelings of the flesh. In these moods of uncertainty, nervous Christians strive to find a mood-lifter. They seek something to force a different mood, as some would take an amphetamine to force a change of mood.

When a Christian cannot attain the mood he desires, he exercises and agitates himself. Then Satan accuses him of not being in right relationship with God and lacking faith. Satan produces some advisers who suggest, as Job's friends did, hidden sin—or perhaps even a lack of salvation. Satan agitates him to seek an experience with God. He makes him think if God loved him He would prove it by giving him the desired feeling. This is the same old trick of Satan, making the Christian doubt that God is faithful and that God is love.

Of course, this lack of a desired feeling raises many doubts: "Is there a hidden sin?" "Am I saved?" "Have I committed the unpardonable sin?" "Maybe I have not worked enough for the Lord."

A patient who did not "have the right feeling" said, "Do I believe? Have I met the conditions laid down in the Word of God? It frightens me when they speak about the Second Coming of Jesus. I wonder if I am ready. Do I really believe? Since I am frightened about death, I must not be saved. My feelings are not right."

Looking Within for a Sign of Assurance

A Christian patient, sincerely desiring help for a condition of long standing, gave this brief history: "I am not Christ-centered, I am self-centered. When my heart palpitates, it makes me think of dying. Then I get panicky, which makes me short of breath. When I get short of breath, I concentrate on dying. Then I wonder if I am saved, because I never had a spiritual experience. A preacher once said, 'Every saved person must have a spiritual experience.' I did not have. I am always worried about myself and I constantly look at my feelings."

It is quite evident that the Christians who go from feeling to feeling have not been growing in the Word. They find one or two passages that are hard to understand and that makes them afraid to search the Scriptures lest they will find more passages that are hard to understand.

A perplexed Christian said, "Is Christ really in my heart? Romans 10:10 bothers me. When I read it I have to say, 'Did I really take Christ in my heart?' What proof do I have? I have no feeling. Satan says, 'You have a good head knowledge, but no heart knowledge—you had better get some assurance!' "

Signs and Compulsions

In desperation a babe in Christ tried to force a feeling by power of concentration and physical exertion. She prayed for a feeling until she was in the throes of a compulsion, compelling her to seek psychiatric relief. She related her problem thus: "If I say 'Lord' in my prayers, I keep repeating it until

83

I get the right feeling. How long should I pray? If I pray as much as I feel I should, I would not find time to take care of my family [she had three preschool children]. Yet the Bible says, 'Pray without ceasing.' I must pray even if I neglect my family."

A certain Christian knew it was wrong to seek and depend on signs, yet he could not refrain. He said, "I was not happy after salvation so I feared I was not saved. I looked for signs. If things worked out for me in a certain way, then Satan said God was in it. By this habit Satan urged me to look for more and more signs instead of going on faith. I finally realized my emptiness toward God at such times. I could not read the Bible, nor could I sing religious songs of praise. It seems I am too aware of my feelings to concentrate on God. I feel too tired to read the Bible, but I am not too tired to follow up some of my signs.

"Too much of this seems to weaken my mind, I cannot think straight. I am so forgetful. I know this is satanic influence on my mind. I cannot explain this to anyone. If I do they might think I am a little off in my mind, which leads me to test my actions to decide if they are from God or from Satan. Soon I catch myself again seeking signs for assurance of God's approval; yet I realize too many of my signs are wishes. There is something uncanny about this. I know for sure it is of Satan because it does not affect my work or social life—only my Christian walk.

"Looking back, I attribute my trouble to hearing other people tell of their vivid experiences in salvation. I had no such experience. I desired an experience for assurance."

I Don't Have the Feeling Others Testify About

Patients troubled with lack of assurance are even more troubled when they attend a testimonial meeting. They are amazed when they hear some of the fiery, vivid, stirring experiences other Christians had when they were saved. Not being grounded in the Word, they conclude they missed something. Either they are not saved or God has bypassed them in not giving them an emotional experience on which they can base salvation.

Satan energized the carnal nature of a nervous Christian to agonize for an experience that would serve him well in a testimonial meeting. He lamented, "I was brought up in a strict Christian home. I have not had any special spiritual experience in my life, such as a vision or being convicted at a revival. I have no assurance. I don't have the feeling others testify about in a testimonial meeting. I try so hard to get it."

Satan gives some individuals a counterfeit. It is feeling in place of faith. But their eyes are not opened to their blindness until the Holy Spirit gets them to see that Christ made the atonement for their souls. They need to believe in the finished work of Christ on the cross of Calvary.

85

One Christian, who lived and suffered for many years under a satanic counterfeit, related this experience: "I am afraid people can look into my eyes and read my thoughts. Glasses seem to help me [the patient always wears dark glasses]. I seem to look from behind something. Why should I hide? I fear I cannot give a sure testimony. I am just parroting what others say. I have no feeling to back it up."

Just Let Go

Christians who have not stabilized themselves in God's Word but depend on their feelings are as unstable as their feelings. They are always in doubt. A certain Christian went to the altar for prayer, seeking assurance of salvation. She desired feelings so she could testify about an experience of salvation. She was told, "Let go of self; let the Spirit have His way."

She said, "I literally let myself go. I was lying on the floor with my arms drawn up. I had orgastic sensations. It was disgusting. I felt sick all over. I know it was not from God. I am afraid to pray alone now because sex thoughts come barging in. When I went to the altar, I hoped for an experience I could get up and tell about in testimonial meetings."

Another Christian with emotional problems wrote: "I have been going to the altar for eight years, wanting this heaviness to leave."

86

The remainder of this patient's letter shows that she was trying to use willpower, which, of course, is self-power. She believed an attitude of utter self-imposed humility should deserve consideration from God, granting her the desired feeling she longs for.

Another Christian explained her problem in these words: "I have gone to the altar again and again, begging the Lord to lift this awful feeling of uncertainty. I dread every evangelistic service because I feel terrible if I do not go up for prayer, but I do not feel any better when I do. I seem to want to tell the whole church how I feel. Maybe that would humble me enough to get rid of my sinful feeling so I can believe."

Another patient stated: "I have gone to the altar off and on so often that I cannot recall the times. I have gone forward and tried for 32 years."

That is 32 years too long! It is pathetic to hear these Christians tell of trying everything but God's Word.

This patient continued, "I tried to discipline my mind by reading typewritten notes of truth while at work, but could retain them no longer than it would take to return them to my purse.

"I must go forward. Perhaps that will give me the joy people talk about. I seem to be all right when I can keep my mind on the Lord. When I look at my doubts, I slip. The people in the church, even the pastor, insist I have some unconfessed sin that hinders my joy. I cannot go to

87

them anymore. I feel ashamed in their presence. I almost wish I had some sin to confess."

Archaeological Christians

Because of persistent urging to look for unconfessed sins, some Christians will even go over their past sins which have been confessed and forgiven. They do this in an honest effort to become truly righteous.

Probing around in sins of the past may harden the conscience to sin for the Christian who has liberal tendencies. Or some zealous Christian may become so obsessed with digging into his past that he becomes a spiritual archaeologist—continually excavating things from his past life.

The drive to dig up the past is energized by Satan, who has beguiled the child of God to strive for a better feeling. This desire to grow in feeling instead of in faith is fleshly (carnal or earthy). It takes the believer away from his faith relationship through the Holy Spirit. The flesh strives against the Spirit of God, and Satan wants to keep the individual in bondage to the flesh.

In his state of bondage to Satan, the person is so wearied from excavating his past at Satan's command that he cannot pause to search the Scriptures to prove that Christ atoned for his sins. Rather, he endeavors to keep himself righteous by his apparent willingness to confess all sins.

Some Christians believe that when memories of past sins come to mind it is a sign that these sins are not forgiven. Satan gives these Christians the absurd idea that when a sin is forgiven it should be blotted out of the person's memory. God never made such a promise. For our comfort and peace, however, He promises that when He forgives us our sins, He will recall them no more: "And will not remember thy sins" (Isa. 43:25); "I will forgive their iniquity, and I will remember their sin no more" (Jer. 31:34).

Satanic Oppression

Satan tries to seduce Christians to lay aside their spiritual armor by getting them to turn to self-occupation with feelings, doubts, works—digging up past sins that are under the blood of Christ. Such Christians wear themselves out. They become exhausted spiritually because they have been so busy hassling with Satan that they neglect to replenish their spiritual strength.

One patient, struggling against Satan, said, "I sometimes wonder if God has forgiven all my sins. Why do they come back and cause me to worry? I do not feel forgiven." From her feelings, this Christian reasons that God will give her a feeling of elation when He is pleased with her and a disquieting feeling when He is displeased with her.

Satan is able to cast a morbid feeling of gloom over some of God's children who are spiritually exhausted. A Christian stated: "I have a feeling something is going to happen. It is a morbid feeling in my chest and head. I cannot describe it so you

89

can understand, but it gives me a fear. This seems to build up until I have the dreadful thought, What if I would commit a morbid act? I might not be able to prevent myself—just like the people the newspapers tell about who commit horrible acts and are written up as being mental."

When many Christians are spiritually exhausted, Satan oppresses them to despair of life. One said, "I get so depressed that I feel like I am about to be buried alive."

Another patient expressed her mood when she said, "Satan has control over me by keeping my attention upon my feelings. I feel I cannot take it any longer, and it seems the way out is to take my life."

Many patients say, "I have never made any attempt to take my life, and I believe I never will because I recognize that this suggestion comes from Satan, and that it is not something that I really want to do."

A patient who recognized the subtlety of Satan said, "Satan is trying to get me to accept his remedy for my situation, but I am not buying it."

Are They Mentally Sick?

It is not unusual for pastors and Christian workers to assume that these Christians in bondage to Satan have "sick minds," because they are so absorbed in their feelings that they cannot be persuaded to read and believe the Bible. They refuse to receive the Word of God for answers to their problems. They cannot or do not believe that the Bible has the solutions to their problems. Yet most of them can read other books and believe what they read.

What makes the difference? The difference is in the authors of the books and Satan's reaction to the Christian's choice of books. Satan does not oppose Christians reading the books of the world because he knows they do not encourage fellowship with God. But Satan also knows that the Word of God has the power to deliver the Christian from his bondage.

It is regretful that even some pastors do not recognize the fact that the patient overcome with his feelings is basically not "mentally" ill, but that he is suffering because of emotional conflict within his soul. He thinks an exalted feeling would be a sign that all is well between him and God.

Well-meaning but ill-informed Christians frequently urge these patients to turn to psychiatry for help. But many Christians who in desperation have turned to non-Christian psychiatry attest to the fact that taking tranquilizers, submitting to insulin shock and electric shock (which have their place), and having the Bible taken away from them because they talked "religion" did not, and could not, relieve them of the anguish of their feelings. None of this delivered them from the bondage of Satan.

A weeping patient said, "In desperation I had two series of electric shock. The second series ended up leaving me with an indifference to God and the Bible. I cannot remember Scripture verses since I had those treatments."

Another nervous Christian who had electric shock said, "I gave up preaching. The Bible is like any other book since I had electric shock."

Still another said, "I lost the spiritual meaning of words. I still lead the choir, but without the realization that this is to glorify God. It is just like a popular tune."

Conclusion

Christians looking for a feeling use feelings in lieu of salvation. It must be made clear to them that when they depend on feelings they are not believing God. Christians must realize that God saves us by grace, not by our works. He does not give us a feeling or a mood. Even sincere Christians are sometimes deceived into thinking that feeling is faith. But feelings are unstable, uncertain, precarious, and as changeable as the weather. As the word "emotion" indicates, it is continually moving and fluctuating. Feelings may even be influenced by our health.

Salvation is not based on feelings, but on the finished work of Christ on Calvary. We are to accept and claim our place as accepted in the Beloved without regard to our inward feelings or emotions. "Therefore being justified by faith, we have peace with God through our Lord Jesus Christ" (Rom. 5:1).

It seems evident from the records and statements of my Christian patients that too much of our preaching stresses, "Raise your hand for prayer," "Come forward." Too often these abbreviated phrases leave out the direct appeal from Him who is calling. Through all this psychological appeal many individuals do not hear because their minds are on what they are urged to do.

Their thoughts are introspecting their emotional reaction to the appeal. They do this instead of centering their eyes on Him who died for them on the cross of Calvary to make an atonement for them.

The Christian in bondage to feelings can be delivered when he keeps his eyes centered on Christ.

Chapter 6
Unbelief

Many Christians with emotional problems suffer because they do not believe God or the Bible. They are constantly harassed by such thoughts as: "I do not know if I believe"; "I do not know if I am saved"; "I am afraid I will not know if I believe"; "How do I know this is not just my wish because others told me?"; "How do I know I let Him into my heart?"; "How can I be sure I believe?"; "How do I know that Christ bore my sins in His own body on the tree?"; "Perhaps I do not have the mental capacity to believe"; "Since I had electric shock I am not sure what I believe"; and finally, "What is believing?"

These Christians are agitated, worried, depressed and driven to utter despair until some even think of taking their lives. One patient said, "I have an urge to destroy myself. Then I get scared thinking what if I were not saved and my believing was just intellectual, which I am almost sure it is. Then I concentrate on 'believe' again until my brain hurts."

These Christians have been frequenting the offices of many pastors and psychiatrists, even traveling great distances, hoping to find some counselor who has the magic charm to "remove the spell." Others keep up a continuous correspondence with various Christian and religious organizations. Even though they receive sound biblical advice, they are unable to apply it to themselves, saying, "That sounds like good advice, but it does not fit my case; mine is different."

One patient, after reading *Nervous Christians*, said, "I decided that my problem was some kind of satanic force no one seemed to understand. So I decided to come to Wichita and find work and stay until I worked it out. My psychiatrist in Washington insisted I go to the state hospital. I knew they could not help me with a spiritual problem."

Believing

I find that many of my patients do not believe their pastor's explanation of salvation through the shed blood of Christ on the cross of Calvary. Yet they will go to a physician, believe his diagnosis for some organic ailment, and follow through with the prescribed treatment. These Christians have no trouble believing what they read in secular books.

Why all this confusion? Are these patients suffering from a mental disorder? Absolutely not! They are not troubled in believing secular knowledge but are only agitated over biblical literature. Is it not logical for non-Christian psychiatry to conclude that if the Bible and things

95

spiritual make these people sick, they should dispense with them? Many patients in desperation for peace try abstaining from all things spiritual; yet they find there is no peace outside of Christ.

Even though these Christian patients resolve to obey their non-Christian psychiatrist while under therapy, invariably they will retain some form of Christian fellowship. One patient with a religious conflict was admonished by his non-Christian psychiatrist not to go to church, Sunday school or revivals. When questioned by his psychiatrist at a later interview, he confessed he was having Bible reading and devotions with his family every morning.

When we consider the fact that these people have their normal mental faculties for secular knowledge, yet are troubled with spiritual facts and words, we realize that it is Satan who enters into the picture, intercepting the spiritual growth of Christians. As babes in Christ they did not feed on the sincere milk of the Word that they might grow thereby (I Pet. 2:2); that they might understand God's plan of redemption for man—that God does it all for us.

God calls us, saves us and seals us. Instead, the unbelieving Christian is afraid he did not do his part in the plan of salvation—as if he had to add a prop to God's plan to hold it up.

Satan gets this type of Christian to dote on the meaning of certain words. This can be best illustrated in the words of a Christian patient who said, "It seems the word 'believe' almost scares me

96

to death. I want to be so sure that I believe that it scares me that maybe I do not. What if God would punish me for doubting so much? This doubting gets me so scared and emotionally upset at times that I nearly go out of my mind. Sometimes when I get this way I wonder if I can go much further. The doubt is constantly with me. I never have a free moment."

Another Christian, who had been in bondage for many years, gave as her reason for not opening the Bible that she was afraid it would stir up too many doubts. During the initial interview this patient said, "Little things bother me so. I have followed the medical instructions rigidly, but I do not get over this. Doctor, it is my nerves. I have had all kinds of nerve medicine. Some make me worse. It started away back there when no one could convince me that I was saved. I am afraid to open my Bible, so I don't.

"I know I am slipping. In times past I wanted to say mean things to people, but I controlled myself. Now it comes out without my being aware of it. Then I am depressed and disgusted, but I cannot apologize. I am so anxious to cooperate with you in order to get over this, but I am afraid I cannot understand or that I will not have the mental capacity. My mind picks up all the doubts, especially when it comes to things about the Bible. I have no trouble reading magazines. I have butterflies in my stomach in your office. I always get that way when I am with Christians. I am afraid

97

I will get snagged on some Bible phrase that will force me to ask myself, Do I believe?"

This patient was convicted of her need for a Saviour and apparently believed, but had been harassed for years with the fear that perhaps she did not fully comprehend the meaning of the word "believe." Many Christians are harassed by Satan with the meaning of words that imply action on the part of the Christian as, "I believe," "I receive," "Work out your salvation."

These Christians do not receive God's salvation by simple faith: "For by grace are ye saved through faith; and that not of yourselves: it is the gift of God: Not of works, lest any man should boast" (Eph. 2:8,9).

These perplexed Christians somehow insist they must have some part—must do something to help God work out their salvation. It is this element of self-work, even in the process of being "born again," that becomes a stumbling block to them. Because they do not yield all of self, Satan seems to encourage them to retain this element of self, which goes forth doing "religious" work instead of first searching the Scriptures and growing on the milk of the Word as all babes in Christ must if they are to grow spiritually.

The child of God who is tormented with the meaning of the words "believe" and "receive" is anxious every time he goes to the house of God, lest the pastor give a call to unbelievers to repent. Immediately these Christians, obsessed with a fear of doubt, become agitated, driven by an urge to go

98

forward to receive Christ—for a certainty once for all. If they resist the urge, they are in torment with thoughts of condemnation—of being hopelessly lost forever. This is truly a condition where Christians are overcome, being in bondage to doubt, because they do not trust God for salvation without man's help.

By this time you have seen the confusion, but where does this problem originate? Just exactly where does Satan enter the scene to stunt the growth of the babe in Christ?

In the Old Testament days the Hebrew people brought an offering to the priest to make an atonement for sins. The Levitical priest placed the sacrifice on the altar without any assistance from the one who brought the offering. This was God's commandment for His children of that day. God's children believed.

On one occasion when serpents entered the camp of the Israelites and many people were bitten, God had Moses raise a brazen serpent on a pole. Those persons who looked to the brazen serpent were healed. Those bitten did not first use some remedy of their own but by faith looked and were healed. In like manner, during the New Testament dispensation God desires that we acknowledge that we are helpless—that He saves us without any help from us. After all, salvation is a miracle. If we can do any part of it, then it is no longer a miracle.

Living faith always lays hold of the living God. The Christian suffering from unbelief is not laying hold of God, but casting about for some reason for assurance rather than having faith in Christ. When God calls us, we are made conscious (convicted) of our sinful, lost state. We realize that we are lost—forever separated from God—unless we accept God's plan of salvation. God will not perform the miracle with our help: "For by grace are ye saved through faith; and that not of yourselves: it is the gift of God: Not of works, lest any man should boast" (Eph. 2:8,9).

God does not ask the drunkard to quit drinking before He saves him. As Christians have observed, the drunkard cannot really stop until after he is saved. God takes away the desire for alcohol when he is washed in the precious blood of Christ.

In like manner, this holds true for the religious man. He cannot give up his religiosity until he has a new nature that gives him a desire for the sincere milk of the Word. This, of course, is true concerning all unsaved, such as the Pharisee, the churchgoer, and the good man—who so often do not see their need of salvation.

When God performs His miracle of salvation, He gives us the faith to believe in Christ as our Saviour: "Looking unto Jesus the author and finisher of our faith" (Heb. 12:2).

We go from faith to faith, and we are "kept by the power of God through faith" (I Pet. 1:5). The faith to believe in Christ is spiritual: "That which is born of the Spirit is spirit" (John 3:6). This is not the faith that is cultivated and acquired by daily experience in the secular realm over which the flesh has control. Spiritual faith grows only as it is exercised in the Word of God.

Deliverance From Bondage

Thank God for His mercy. Not all nervous Christians who are overcome by Satan remain in bondage to him a whole lifetime. Fortunately, many of these Christians are delivered from their unbelief.

One patient, a Bible student who was delivered, summed up his experience as follows: "When I was first saved I had a lot of religiosity. I had wagonloads of religion, but it did not express the love of Christ. I had no standard to go by but my own. I had my own rules of salvation, which were moral rules laid down by my parents. Even after I claimed I believed in Jesus, I still adhered to my unsaved parents' doctrinal teachings. I was guilty of measuring all my actions by their moral measuring stick.

"I was a zealous driver for souls for the Lord. I gave out tracts on street corners. I would feel compelled to stay out at night until two or three o'clock in the morning, talking to people about salvation. I had a lot of arguments, but no love. My pastor always preaches negative sermons just like my folks—'don't, don't, don't'—but gives me nothing positive. I had a rough time in Bible school the first year. By the second year, the doubts about my salvation left me after I was taught to digest the whole Bible, not just isolated verses."

Salvation, Joy, Testing

Even Christians who come for psychiatric help testify of the joy they experienced when they were washed in the precious blood of Jesus Christ and sealed with the Holy Spirit.

Inevitably, when the time of testing sets in, Satan sends dark clouds and an oppressive atmosphere, disrupting the joy and peace. If the Christian is not clad in the garment of protection, as described in the sixth chapter of Ephesians, he will not be able "to stand against the wiles of the devil" (v. 11). However, all babes in Christ must learn sooner or later that the Christian life is not a bed of roses and that God does not promise to keep His children out of the storms and stresses of life. He does, however, give His children strength and protection to endure the storms as they draw their strength from Him.

Doubt and Anxiety

Satan enters the scene when he finds, or creates for himself, the psychological setting best suited for his purpose. With his time-honored weapon of doubt, he approaches the Christian. Then the Christian finds himself in gloom or heaviness—he is confused. Because he has a letdown feeling, he believes there must be sin in his life and that God has forsaken him.

Satan suggests that perhaps he was never saved—that maybe he is not a child of God. This doubt creates an anxiety and makes the Christian search himself. Satan causes these Christians to ask themselves: "How was I saved?" "How do I know I believed?" "Did I accept Him, did I receive Him, and did I believe at the time I received Him?"

One patient was even tormented with thoughts about humility: "Do I feel this way because I held my head up instead of hanging it down in humility when I was baptized? I just cannot put my finger on my sin. If I am really saved and do not know it, how will I know in the future? Doctor, please tell me, is my mind all right? Am I capable of believing?"

By this bewildered reasoning the child of God takes his mind completely off what Christ did for him on Calvary. He seems to forget that Christ did it *all* for him, and he simply should receive by grace what Christ did for him. He does not need to exercise himself about the word "believe."

Truly, these Christians know that "fear hath torment" (I John 4:18). They are in a whirlpool of doubt, and they cannot get out. Their thoughts are all tied to this obsession. Usually they are afraid to look into the Bible lest they add more doubts. They go to church with much fear and trepidation lest they hear statements that might shatter what little faith they have. While in the church service, they become more anxious as the service nears the close. Should they go forward when an invitation is given for the lost? Especially is this critical when the appeal is made emphasizing that all you need to do is "believe." This makes them conscious of the fact that they must do something. They must

103

believe instead of centering the whole weight of conversion on what Christ did for them through His precious blood on Calvary.

One Christian, perplexed and driven by doubt, gave his experience thus: "I used to enjoy going to church, but not anymore. I read my Bible but have a guilty feeling that perhaps I do not believe as strongly as I should; that perhaps I have an unwilling spirit, a spirit of unbelief.

"Then I get busy to offset this fear by doing more Boy Scout work in the church and by attending all the meetings in the church. There is something going on almost every night, which leaves me no time with my family and, incidentally, no time for Bible reading, which I guess I deliberately avoid in my present mental state.

"Satan turns my zeal into works until I am very tired, and yet the fear that I have not done enough for the Lord remains with me. This fear and anxiety about the Lord, plus my tired and tense bodily symptoms, make a wreck of me. I just seem to get unbalanced. What I do for the Lord the Devil drives me to overdo. I have now arrived at this crucial point. In the past my doubts all centered around God, the Bible and my church. Now I find the doubt entering my work, interfering with my earning a livelihood."

Christians who doubt are always in difficulty. They may be reading a chapter in the Bible which deals with the Christian's walk. When they come across a phrase that deals with punishment for disobedience or the withholding of rewards, their minds immediately revert to pre-salvation days when their parents exacted obedience to their rules of conduct by warning that misconduct and ill behavior would keep them out of heaven.

These Christians have no peace because of their off-and-on faith. Misinterpreted Bible verses can cast a gloom that endures for days and months. This is all because these people do not realize what their position is in Christ: "There is therefore now no condemnation to them which are in Christ Jesus" (Rom. 8:1).

When first saved, these Christians have joy and perhaps all goes well while they are in Christian fellowship. But when dark clouds gather, they meditate about possible indwelling sin. This brings on wondering thoughts, reasonings and questionings. Then what becomes of faith? Unbelief sets in. Then follow doubt, anxiety, fear, despondency and self-pity. Many will say during such times, "God has forsaken me. He does not hear my prayers."

It is not that God has forsaken His child, but rather that His child—by his own reasonings and unbelief—has turned to self-pity.

Satan Battles Mind With Psychology

Christians cannot avoid all the psychological reasonings of these last days. They will succumb to some of the malicious influences unless they keep their eyes centered on Christ. Christians who are not Christ-centered will have some areas of their lives open for satanic attack.

Satan may approach in one of two ways. He may slyly enter the mind (thinking) of those Christians who depend on reasoning and psychologies of man by urging them to "think positively"; "push out evil thoughts"; "determine to have a clean mind"; "keep sin out of your life."

A troubled Christian wrote: "I read a book by a noted evangelist who is well known for his writings. He wrote that it is up to you to keep sin out of your life (mind). Before that time I went in grace. That statement made me feel it was up to me to keep my mind set against sin. Instead of turning to the Bible, I read more books on how to control my thinking, until I was harassed even in my dreams with evil thoughts against Jesus."

Another Christian with emotional problems wrote: "I am tormented by negative thoughts such as, I do not want Christ. Then the thoughts come that I have committed the unpardonable sin; that I am not saved; that I have no chance to be saved. I seem to go from one obsession to another.

"This came over me after I had some conflicts with myself over whether I could do certain things that Christians should not do. Before I was saved I danced, did some acting, and I loved it. I was tempted of the flesh to do it again and tried to reason with myself that God would not care."

By her reasonings, Satan used her mind to battle against God. This increased until she turned to commune with God and meditated on the

106

power of the shed blood of Christ on Calvary. She was then victorious through Christ.

Another Christian, who was overwhelmed with mental confusion before he was willing to turn from his doubts and believe in what Christ did for him, said, "During my mental upheaval, or nervous breakdown as some called it, I was attacked by an unbelievable sex temptation. It was a demonic urge of sexual desire for other women, even though I am married and a Christian. During this weak period, Bible reading and prayer had no power over the demonic urge.

"I made several attempts at different times to get psychiatric help. I was urged to talk it out, and some psychiatrists gave me tranquilizers. Talking it out made a terrible conflict for me. I was worse. It built up more of an urge. They gave me no help. They kept ignoring my spiritual convictions. I am hoping you will not want to hear all the filth that has filled my mind for the past several years."

This patient was entirely correct in not wanting to rehearse the evil imaginations. Free association and catharsis are not the cure for the Christian's spiritual problems. Nor can tranquilizers make the problems disappear. The Christian must, as this Christian did, look to Christ who is our sin-bearer. He overcame doubt and demonic urges when he learned to fully appreciate the verses which tell of the power of Christ's blood to deliver. The verses dealing with Christ's atonement took away the doubts which had been hindering his spiritual growth.

This patient, like most Christian patients suffering from unbelief, had the beginning of his trouble soon after he was saved. Invariably, these Christians have joy for a period after they are saved. Somehow they seem satisfied with this experience. They neglect taking the proper spiritual nourishment as soon as they are saved; that is, studying to learn more about the blessed Lord who redeemed them and gave them the inner joy. They may testify of their joy, but this does not endure because of their lack of feasting on the Word. It is during this period of negligence and malnutrition that self and Satan try to reason out salvation by the reasonings of man. This is impossible. Spiritual things cannot be reasoned by man's intellect. They are understood by the faith of the Son of God.

Perhaps you ask, "Why do Christians with emotional problems turn back to the psychological reasonings of man? Why do they not submit to God and resist the Devil?"

They cannot because they are suffering from spiritual malnutrition and have no strength. Just as our physical bodies need proper nourishment to develop and grow in strength, we acquire spiritual strength by feeding on a spiritual diet—the Word of God.

Unless Christians *first* submit to God, they are powerless against the wiles of the Devil. We learn to submit to God's will and live in obedience to Him by meditating on His Word, the Bible.

108

Christians with emotional problems do not read the Word of God because they are afraid they will find words or passages that will add fuel to the fire of doubt; therefore, they do not have spiritual knowledge, spiritual understanding or spiritual strength.

Because of their constant doubts, these Christians have no rest. They are in continual emotional turmoil day and night. Their spiritual conflicts, anxieties, doubts and fearful introspection are evidences of divine life within. Although they may be saved and have peace with God, they do not have "the peace of God, which passeth all understanding" (Phil. 4:7). They lack this peace because they have not appropriated all that grace includes. They cannot enjoy the blessings of the abundant life because they do not have the assurance of salvation.

Nervous Christians who live in unbelief feel frustrated and defeated.

Chapter 7
Compulsion and Restitution

One of the most distressing problems that Christian patients bring to me is the irresistible compulsion to make a restitution to release an anxiety.

The symptom is an inner, inexplainable urge or compulsion, distracting the patient's thoughts from the problem at hand. The agitation is a harassment that comes to the conscious mind as a floating anxiety. One might say he has a guilty conscience that gives him no peace. Usually it is awakened and stimulated when the Christian faces or is anticipating a situation which creates for him a guilt feeling. For this feeling he makes a confession or an appropriate restitution, which seems to allay the anxiety over the guilt momentarily.

The floating anxiety seems to come, as all these patients say, "from nowhere in particular." Yet it seems to be triggered by specific moods when performing certain tasks that create anxiety. Since the mood is unpleasant (painful) they seek relief, which in times past has been accomplished by making a restitution to appease the anxiety.

Origin of Compulsive Restitution

This old self-nature in the Christian, which has not been reckoned crucified, is a part of the old self-nature that served to appease the guilty conscience in the days before salvation. Since self has not been counted or reckoned crucified, dead and buried, it is easy for Satan to use it for his purposes—to keep the Christian bound to his old habit.

The self-nature seems ever to be open to this intruding spirit that comes to the mind to create a guilty sensation, interfering with the work at hand. It is so persistent in its demand that the individual, rather than being wearied by its continuous demand, pauses to make a confession or restitution to appease this compulsive spirit. The compulsive drives of the self-nature to find release can never be satisfied. Self can never be satisfied. The Christian, driven by compulsion, is never free of his torment until he deals with the old self.

One Christian said, "In times past I felt utterly condemned, especially after a bout with masturbation. Confession or restitution relieved me momentarily. Therefore, whenever I felt condemned or guilty from any cause, I would try to find some flimsy basis on which to make a restitution. The restitution or confession gave me a sense of relief—a release from that oppressive feeling of condemnation. Finally, making restitution became a habit whenever I felt condemned for anything I did that I felt might be corrected or possibly improved. This eventually made restitution meaningless as far as what it was supposed to accomplish for my soul.

"When I was saved I continued to be controlled by the desire to make a confession to appease that anxiety I have. Even though I know what Christ's suffering on the cross means for me, I can't seem to put my trust in His finished work. I feel driven to do something myself to release this anxiety."

Satanic Influence

Satan drives this type of Christian to introspect his subconscious thoughts, to check himself to see if he has done his best to fulfill his part in his program of self-righteousness. He has been ensnared by Satan to add his self-righteous concept of salvation, which he established before he was saved, to God's salvation when he was born from above. This serves as a form of double assurance. Nevertheless, the old self-righteous salvation principle dominates his life, and the salvation through Christ's atoning work on Calvary is relegated to the background.

Such patients know God saves, yet their subconscious minds, influenced by Satan, urge them to live by their own righteous standards to which they were enslaved before salvation. Satan shortchanged them by intercepting their growth in the grace of our Lord Jesus so that they have no joy and no living faith in the Lord. He causes them to adhere to the old self-standards they lived by

112

before they were saved. He tantalizes them by accusing them, when they are in the throes of an anxious mood, of not living perfectly before God.

The perfection they aspire to is not to please God, but to appease the guilty mood of not being satisfied with their own accomplishments. At first Satan suggests, but later demands, that they must be more exact—even perfect—if they wish to please God and have the joy of salvation as evidenced in the lives of their fellow Christians.

Influenced by Satan, they resolve with renewed effort to be scrupulously honest—yes, perfect! The plaguing thought comes: Have I done my best? By repeating the act or work, couldn't it be improved? If there is a remote possibility of improvement, they feel they should repeat it. The result is that they keep repeating it until a compulsive ritual has been established, which rules their lives day by day.

A Christian who had suffered all his adult life with a compulsion said, "Ever since I have been saved I go back and make restitution for many things. Since I am saved I know I should claim His victory for my life and be free of my bondage, but I have no peace and no joy. I know this is not right for a Christian."

This patient was obsessed with the fear that his car was contaminated with TB germs. He said, "My uncle lived in our home; he died of TB two years ago. He never sat in my car, but I fear I have carried TB germs into my car on my clothes. I washed the car on the inside several times with

113

Lysol. I am afraid to sell it, lest someone buy it and contract TB."

He had come to the point that he could not stay on a job very long because of his fear of contaminating people, even though he wore new clothes and washed his hands so many times a day that they were raw. He was trying to find proper medical care for the dermatitis on his hands, which he had brought upon himself by too much washing.

Why the fear of TB? Why the urge for constant hand-washing?

In his youth, many years before his conversion, he had no way of being cleansed of a guilty conscience for having committed incest with his sister. The guilt remained with him daily for years. He would promise himself he would not yield to the lust again, and he would wash his hands many times as a method of self-ablution.

This did not cleanse his conscience. The consequent hand-washing gradually became a pattern of self-cleansing for sin whenever he felt guilty—not only for incest in his youth but also for a guilty conscience related to his daily life, such as giving others proper change and checking back on former visits to see if he had made enemies.

This Christian, like many others with his type of suffering, knew his standing in Christ and believed that Christ had redeemed him with His shed blood on the cross of Calvary. But these Christians cannot apply I John 1:9 because they are bound by their compulsive habits.

Satan continues to hold them in bondage to the reasoning that they must add their own restitution and compulsive rituals to what Christ has done. This reasoning, of course, continues to hold them in bondage to the uncrucified self, which Satan can energize whenever the compulsive Christian senses guilt.

When we say "bondage" we mean they cannot refrain from their compulsive acts. They would if they could because they do not enjoy the agitated, restless inner coercion.

At first these ritualistic habits may be centered around one or more phases of the Christian's life in which he had been particularly zealous. Eventually the energizing spirit makes him self-righteously zealous about many things in his daily walk. Especially is this so if the problem is related to or based on some guilt for which the Christian did not know how to turn to God for forgiveness—either before or after he became a Christian.

Here is what one Christian said about his battle with restitution: "When I was a boy and told a lie, I would go to my mother and confess and she forgave me. I was relieved. I was so happy after the forgiveness. I felt that when she forgave me, God also forgave me and I was again fit for heaven.

"When I have an anxious feeling now as an adult, it seems I yearn for the experience of being able to go to Mother to confess something or to do something to please her which would give me a happy feeling and dispel this anxiety—sort of a feeling that Mother loves me again and I don't have

115

to be anxious and afraid of her disapproval. But now it is God's approval I yearn for.

"This anxiety stays with me until I find something I can do that gives me a lift. I seem compelled to perform some act of restitution. If I am doubtful about some statement I made, I make some excuse to open the subject in a sly way to have the individual assure me I was right and that he was pleased with me. Then I have a feeling that all is right again—like my boyhood experience when I confessed to Mother and she graciously accepted my confession. It made me feel good because Mother loved me again. Before my confession I felt she could not love me—a bad boy."

This Christian does not always make restitution to satisfy a desire of repentance. He is satisfying a subconscious, infantile desire to be loved again.

Some time later this Christian made the following statement: "Since I now understand how this had its inception, I can turn to the Lord and assure myself that Christ did it all; that I had no part in saving myself; that I cannot do anything to add to my salvation. As I think on what He did for me, eventually the agitation leaves me. It is gradually disappearing."

Restitution and Satan

Restitution can become a satanic illusion. The Christian steeped in restitution truly believes he is zealously serving the Lord. He has convinced himself that he is working to be pleasing to the Lord. It is an illusion because he does not realize that the more he serves restitution, the more unspiritual he becomes. He finds less time to read God's Word. When he does read the Bible, he searches for Bible verses to fortify his principle of restitution.

When Satan has his victim thus occupied, he congratulates himself because he sees how successful he has been in enticing one of God's would-be zealous workers away from praising and worshiping God. Satan wears him out physically and mentally on a false doctrine—a do-it-yourself program: "You must keep yourself sinless to be saved."

None of these Christians are at peace, nor do they ever have a sense of joy after the various acts of restitution. This is because these acts are not carried out by the motivation of the Holy Spirit but by a self-desire. The purpose is not to help the other person but to please the ego of the one making restitution.

They may become weary of being driven by their taskmaster, the Deceiver, but he always has another gimmick to stimulate his workers. Quite often some Christians, who are not well-grounded in the meaning of Christ's atoning work, are driven to make restitution for some nonsensical things after hearing testimonies stressing restitution. In fact, some Christians have periodic compulsions to make restitution.

117

When it does not result from a motive of love, restitution becomes simply a satanic diversion. One Christian, after being delivered from his bondage, made this observation: "Restitution as a duty does you no good. When restitution is carried out with a love motive, it is a New Testament restitution. Only restitution with love brings peace to the soul."

Restitution is seldom a serious problem for the spiritual Christian. He realizes that *all* of his sins have been forgiven, not just some. He knows that all of his sins have been paid for by the blood of Christ.

The Christian needs only to remind himself of his identification with Christ in His crucifixion, death, burial and resurrection. He is to reckon self as set aside and to walk moment by moment in the power of Christ.

Christians tied to restitution are not trusting Christ's finished work. They keep returning to their past. However, the Apostle Paul said, "Forgetting those things which are behind, and reaching forth unto those things which are before, I press toward the mark for the prize of the high calling of God in Christ Jesus" (Phil. 3:13,14).

Chapter 8

Self-Righteousness

While reminiscing, one of my patients said, "At the age of 11 I thought I was living an obedient life, but I had not been baptized. I never understood the meaning of a new life until I got confused and had to seek help."

Many nervous patients suffer because they do not depend on God to save them. Instead, they depend on their self-righteousness to save them. With their mouths they confess that Jesus saves sinners from hell. Because they do not want to go to hell with lost sinners, they give assent to the idea that they want to be saved from hell. Somehow it never occurs to them that people who are good, moral and upright should be considered as lost as "the fearful, and unbelieving, and the abominable, and murderers, and whoremongers, and sorcerers, and idolaters, and all liars, [that] shall have their part in the lake which burneth with fire" (Rev. 21:8).

These patients admit that it was necessary for Jesus to die for such wicked sinners. However, it is an offense to their decent, moral standards to have

119

to acknowledge that they also are included in Romans 3:22,23: "For there is no difference: For all have sinned, and come short of the glory of God." It seems unreasonable to these people to consider themselves sinners along with morally degraded individuals.

The Call to Receive Jesus

When the invitation to receive Jesus is given from the pulpit, those with high moral standards are in a quandary about going forward when they are convicted of their need. They want to be saved from hell and go to heaven, but they are afraid of what others will think. One person said, "If I go forward the people will see I am a sinner. What sin will they think I am guilty of? Perhaps they will think I am a homosexual because the evangelist bore down on that sin in his message. I would die if they thought that of me. I dread the thought because I am afraid some people think that of me already, because I am 40 years old and not married."

Another said, "I hesitated a long time before I went forward. I was afraid I would break down and weep before the whole congregation. This would have annoyed my father. He is not given to emotional demonstrations. Furthermore, Father would have been ashamed of me had I wept for my sins. He would have felt that people would look down on him as a delinquent father for having reared such a terrible sinner. I did not let myself

120

weep when I was saved. I wanted to and I have been uncomfortable about it ever since. That is why I made this long trip to see you."

After this Christian was able to get his eyes off self and his concern off what others thought, he had joy in what Christ did for him. He realized that his own moral rules were a hindrance to his having fellowship with Christ. Later, he made this confession: "Now I am not ashamed to weep. I have repented of my self-righteous religion."

Satan's Counterfeit for Salvation—Self-Righteousness

Satan offers to the moral, self-righteous individual a psychology that will appeal to his type of personality. Satan, the master psychologist, knows the reasonings of man. He knows that his moral, self-righteous victim will cling to his cloak of self-righteousness, but Satan will not object to religion and high moral standards. This should not seem strange to us. Satan comes as an angel of light, constantly endeavoring to counterfeit God's program. While deceiving them, Satan encourages those who are untrained in the Bible to form their own standards of religion. High moral standards are pleasing to Satan as long as Christ's redemptive work on Calvary is left out.

Satan controls the lives of the unsaved, for they belong to him and are called "the children of disobedience" (Eph. 2:2). When the unsaved become God-conscious and make an effort to pattern their lives after some Christians, Satan

121

comes to their aid by offering them an imitation of godliness. In this way he hopes to divert them from thinking about their lost state.

After hearing a sermon, one Christian explained, "The evangelist said, 'God will do His part; you must do your part.' " This suggested to him that he had to exercise his willpower to live up to the moral standards he had set for himself.

Another Christian patient said, "I hesitated a long time before I went forward and accepted Christ. I worried and wondered if I could live up to it. I did not want to commit myself to live the standard I was supposed to live."

A patient who tried to live up to the rules and regulations of the church said, "I knew I was lost. I was afraid to join their church because I was afraid I could not live up to it. They convinced me. I was baptized into that church. I thought if I lived up to the rules I was a good Christian. Now I see that the rules worried me. I did not study my Bible. I would say, 'Jesus saves,' but I did not realize that He did it all and the rules were my own."

Measuring Themselves by Themselves

"When we follow the righteous yardstick we established in childhood, we are influenced by it in adult life even when saved," confessed a patient who had overcome Satan and discarded his self-righteous yardstick.

The patient made other statements which indicated he had acquired a clear comprehension of

122

the problem which he had presented: "Satan strives to make us establish our own rules of righteousness, which is really rebellion against God, and to make us trust in ourselves. Then our minds are not on God. We are not worshiping God; we are going in our own strength. God wants us to keep our eyes on Him, not on the things of the world or on man-made rules."

When this patient came to me for help he was constantly tormented by anxiety, wondering if he was abiding by his personal yardstick. He cherished his yardstick because it was his very own measuring standard, made up of some disconnected Bible thoughts, church doctrine and his self-imposed moral standards. He judged, criticized and condemned other Christians by his standards.

Satan had this patient so completely bound to his self-made yardstick that he took no interest in Bible reading. It did not occur to him to search the Scriptures to see if his yardstick was in accordance to God's standard. If he had read the Apostle Paul's second letter to the Corinthians, he would have found his condition diagnosed in chapter 10, verse 12: "But they measuring themselves by themselves, and comparing themselves among themselves, are not wise." He would have found the remedy for his condition in verses 17 and 18: "But he that glorieth, let him glory in the Lord. For not he that commendeth himself is approved, but whom the Lord commendeth."

By the time the patient came for psychotherapy, Satan had already blinded him, bound

123

him and caused him to look at only himself. Over a period of several years, his anxiety had grown because he realized he was falling short of his desire to measure up to the yardstick he had established for himself. Satan overcame this Christian, who was basically conscientious about his ego standards. Satan goaded him on to become more perfect in his own eyes—driving him harder and harder—until he became so anxious that he had to seek psychiatric help for release from his anxiety.

Training and Legalism

After salvation many babes in Christ set up standards which seem good to them. But what is Christian and what is not Christian? What must the Christian do and what must he not do? Usually, the standard set up is a moral or religious code drilled into the person during his growing years. When he fails in his resolution, he very often believes he has lost his salvation. This is based on the false teaching that getting into heaven depends on being obedient to the discipline of his parents: "If you are not good, you will not get into heaven. God does not take sinners, such as naughty boys, into heaven. You will have to go to the place where bad boys go."

When this false teaching has been nurtured in the child, it comes back to haunt the newborn child of God as a necessary addition to salvation.

124

Especially is this true when the wrath of God has been emphasized apart from the love of God.

Many people who have been reared on this false teaching do accept the way of salvation through the shed blood of Christ, but they strive to live by the old moral code of ethics taught in childhood.

One patient, who became frustrated because his obsessive conduct no longer gave him peace, held his bowed head between his hands and wept, saying, "Now what will I do? I don't know what to do. I wish I had never asked anyone about my compulsions. They didn't help me anyway."

The non-Christian psychiatrist whom this patient had consulted diagnosed him as "a case suffering from too much religion" and advised him to refrain from Bible reading and all church activities.

A patient whose fuzzy comprehension of salvation and righteousness had caused her much heartache explained her suffering in this way: "I make rules and then force myself to follow them. The rules I make are harder for me to follow than the Lord's rules. I make myself miserable by my rules."

The self-righteous Christian who was reared on rules and regulations makes a rule and says, "I will follow this rule." Then he comes to the decision that he is obedient, righteous and honest as long as he adheres to the tenets of this rule. His conscience tells him that he is obedient and faithful to God because he does not deviate from the rule. If

125

circumstances cause him to do so, he fears God will punish him for breaking the rule. What rule? Whose rule? God's rule? No! God had no part in establishing such a rule.

But why the rule? There seems to be an inherent need for man to follow a rule or law. He has a need to be governed. Even if he has to make the rule or the law himself, he seeks to be disciplined. Because his self-made rules of discipline have a semblance of godly righteousness, he is deceived into believing that they have heavenly approval.

A code of do's and don'ts may in itself be commendable, but we are not saved by man-made rules and regulations: "For by grace are ye saved through faith; and that not of yourselves: it is the gift of God" (Eph. 2:8).

Another Christian had this to say about the struggle with his self-made measuring stick: "I am very righteous. Satan is trying to have me self-righteous. I seem to want to resist what I hear that is contrary to my principles, even if it comes from the Bible. In fact, I listen with an attitude that wants to resist other Christians who want to help me. I seem to be guarding my rules of self-righteousness. It irritates me when they open the Bible and show me Scripture passages that contradict what I believe. It scares me. It takes away my sense of assurance. Then I do not have anything! What can I believe?"

The man who bases his salvation on his self-righteousness is easily upset when he hears an

126

evangelistic appeal or receives a tract intended for the unsaved. The Holy Spirit seems to convict him that his self-made measuring stick might fall short of what the Bible teaches. This creates an uneasiness in the self-nature and causes doubts, feelings of pride, envy, despair, anxiety, obsessions, fanaticism, suicide tendencies; in fact, all the carnal exponents of the selfhood. He seems to be alerted to guard his self-made righteous measuring stick. He is ready to challenge any attempt to disprove his righteousness.

Saved But Self-Righteous

Satan makes his approach very early in the new life of the babe in Christ. Almost immediately after the Holy Spirit has called the person into God's family, Satan attempts to assure him that he can be saved and keep himself saved only by self-effort. This creates a stumbling block for many who are convicted of sin but who fear they cannot live up to the standards of the Christian life.

Even though they know that Jesus saves, they must add their legalism for a feeling of assurance. These Christians are usually carried away by their emotions. They strive continually for a feeling. They go from feeling to feeling instead of from faith to faith (Rom. 1:17). Satan has deceived them into believing that as long as they have a good feeling, all is well with their souls. Satan is able to influence them and give them certain

127

feelings while their self-natures are busily occupied upholding the self-righteous measuring stick.

For such people, daily living is a striving to live up to the "standard" in order to maintain salvation. They are determined to live by their self-devised legalism, and they expect God to add His grace and mercy to their legalism. God cannot do this.

Self-righteous patients who depend on their own standards seem to forget grace. The "self," which makes them self-righteous, must be on the alert lest they lose their salvation. One lady said, "I must keep my eyes on the Lord at all times. If I do not I could end up in hell, because the Bible says if we are not careful, the Devil will devour us as a roaring lion." At another time she said, "How can I have salvation and not be perfect?" This patient was not quoting Scripture but excerpts from her self-imposed standards, which had a biblical flavor.

While working in a shop with a group of fellow Christians, this patient shared the privilege of drawing money out of a petty cash account. This account had been set up as a convenience for anyone in need of emergency cash for such things as lunch and bus fare. On one occasion, after she had neglected to return her withdrawal, she said to a fellow employee, "I had better get that money paid back into the box. If I were to die today, I would go to hell because God knows I took the money and have not paid it back."

Self-centered Christians, in bondage to their self-righteous standards, are not aware that they

128

are out of fellowship with Christ and are living by self-effort. They sincerely believe their religious activities have God's approval and that they are working for the Lord. Satan drives them to improve themselves to attain greater heights of achievement—all by self-effort—until they are driven by a demon of perfectionism, scrupulosity, restitution and fanaticism.

There are many types and degrees of perfectionism that end up in the psychiatrist's consultation room. In all cases the patients inflict their own suffering by their own self-made rules. Not only does this type of Christian suffer the torment of invisible demons but—being spiritually maladjusted—he also makes God's people suffer with him. To the unsaved, his religious compulsiveness is just considered "religious fanaticism."

Self-Standard and Formality of Accepting Jesus

Those who have been converted have repented from their unregenerate state of rebellion against God. However, Christians suffering from phobias, compulsions, self-centeredness, restitution and perfectionism seldom talk about repentance and conversion—even though they testify they are saved.

Because many self-righteous Christians have been reared in strictly disciplined religious homes, they have adjusted to a moral, ethical code of behavior. It is not unusual to hear these Christians

129

testify that they received Christ on a certain date. However, some have only added Jesus to their self-made righteous standard for good measure. Instead of going on and growing in Christ, they continue to live in their self-righteousness.

A carnal Christian said, "During sermons I listened for things that had to do with righteousness so that I could improve myself. I remembered the examples given about spiritual giants. I wanted to imitate their exploits. That is what I thought was a successful Christian. I never realized what salvation was. I was trying to be perfect as far as the church taught. I tried to live perfectly before the people."

Some self-righteous Christians are versatile enough to adjust their self-righteous standards to the times and situations. They separate themselves from the world, but their separation is not unto God. They are worldly enough to suit the world and not Christlike enough to offend the world. They let the world alone and the world lets them alone. They have not lost their taste for the things of the world, but their self-righteous indignation sets up a straw man of specific sins against which they crusade.

Satan will not molest these self-righteous Christians because they are not disturbing his program. Their works are not dedicated to the glory of God but are inspired by their self-righteous zeal, which is motivated by self. Yet they have no joy and peace because they are not resting on the finished work of Christ.

130

Self-Righteous Workers

Some Christians do not seem to get into trouble until they attempt to lead others to the knowledge of the saving grace of Christ through His shed blood on Calvary. They may do all kinds of religious works as long as conversion and salvation are not emphasized.

Two young ladies, with much zeal about doing the Lord's work, were suddenly made to think seriously one day. They were leading a class of children in singing, "Open your heart and let Him in." When they asked the children if they had taken Jesus into their hearts, the positive, sincere response shocked them. They became convicted in their hearts and had to ask themselves if they had really received Jesus as Saviour.

They did not have assurance of salvation because they were not established in the Word. Their self-righteous moral standards could not assuage the doubts. In both workers the doubts increased to such intensity that they had to seek psychiatric help because they were harassed with the fear of losing their minds if the doubts continued.

Self-righteous Christians are conspicuous among the body of believers, constantly attracting attention to themselves. They run everywhere, beseeching the pastor, the visiting evangelist and the many self-styled counselors concerning their doubts. They seldom find enduring answers because the answers do not seem to dovetail into their self-made righteousness. Frequently, they add to their dilemma by incorporating false doctrine into their legalistic standards. Even church doctrine is sometimes put on a level with the Bible.

A number of patients have presented me with books setting forth their church doctrine, saying, "This is what we believe." Their church doctrine takes precedence over biblical teaching. They complain, "No one understands me because people cannot understand what I believe." They are so bound to their frustrations they cannot have open minds to receive help. I am not as concerned about what the patient's church believes as I am about what the patient believes. I am treating the patient, not the church.

Self-righteousness is carnality. Carnal Christians are more concerned about their desires than they are about pleasing Christ. They may recognize Christ, but their desires revolve around self: "Measuring themselves by themselves and comparing themselves among themselves" (II Cor. 10:12).

A Christian whose salvation is colored and influenced by a subconscious legalism is self-conscious instead of Christ-conscious. His legalistic righteousness controls his actions, his thinking and his life.

Chapter 9

I Want to Work for the Lord

Many of my patients have a zeal for religious works: "I want to work for the Lord"; "I want to be used of the Lord"; "I want to be in the Lord's will"; "I want to be in the Lord's service"; "I want to be used of the Lord to do great things for Him"; "I want to give my all for the Lord; the Bible says to surrender your life."

"I want to work for the Lord. If only He would deliver me of my fatigue," said one nervous patient, who suffered from a state of exhaustion when she learned that her children had joined a religious cult. The bitterness and disappointment made her tense and utterly discouraged, resulting in her being put to bed suffering from so-called nervous exhaustion.

The patient complained, "I am ashamed to witness since my children turned out as they did. In this fatigued state I am not a good testimony for Christ. The worry about my children is like a curtain over my mind. If I could work for the Lord, I could forget the bitterness and disappointment."

133

A carnal Christian, active in all kinds of church activities, said, "I was hoping that if I worked for the Lord, He would take away the anxious thoughts about myself."

Another patient, reasoning along the same line, expressed herself thus: "I thought if I kept myself very busy with church work and working for the Lord, I would get away from my fears of being abnormal."

These patients want to know why "working for the Lord" does not take away their undesirable feelings and give them joy. They do not realize that the undesirable feelings should be overcome *before* they attempt to work for the Lord. Too often the urge to "work for the Lord" is self-inspired to atone for sin; to soothe a guilty conscience; to divert a mind from multitudinous fears. Such things cannot be accomplished by works.

Of course, Satan is the deceiver in this problem. One Christian said, "Satan deceived me by turning my zeal into works, but I should have been resting in the Lord and communing with Him. In my anxiety to serve Him, I neglected my Bible reading and even prayer. I expected my works to give me peace, love and joy, but they only brought on more conflicts. Satan really tricked me to get my eyes off the Lord and on self."

Many carnal Christians never realize that their zeal for working for the Lord is an ego drive to gratify self and not to glorify God. They may read or even quote Galatians 2:20: "I am crucified with Christ: nevertheless I live; yet not I, but Christ liveth in me: and the life which I now live in the flesh I live by the faith of the Son of God, who loved me, and gave himself for me." However, the spiritual application does not seem to dawn upon them. The ego is not dethroned and reckoned crucified, dead and buried with Christ. It is a simple matter for carnal Christians to quote Bible verses which have powerful spiritual meaning without themselves having experienced any of that power and meaning!

Religious Works Cover

Many Christians who say they want to work for the Lord really mean they want to do religious works. These are not works for the Lord but works for self. They have a self-reason for their zeal to work. But does their zeal glorify Christ?

Our zeal should be like the zeal of John and Peter who said, "For we cannot but speak the things which we have seen and heard" (Acts 4:20).

One Christian patient said, "I attended a Bible-study group. I did not feel I knew as much as the people in the group. I felt uncomfortable so I got out. I did not want them to find out how little I knew about the Bible. I had an urge to be in the Lord's work; I wanted to be a leader. I turned to children's work because they did not know how little I knew, and they did not criticize me."

It is true that children may not be bold enough to outwardly criticize the worker, but they are not

135

easily deceived. They know when a worker does not really love the Lord.

Later the patient said, "It seems I had to come to my present mental confusion to see that self had not been reckoned crucified. Daily I was seeking approval, praise and encouragement from people instead of glorifying God."

Many may even engage in personal work or some form of religious work while their lives remain full of things displeasing to God. The presence of those displeasing things hinders God's blessings upon their work. Too often, if they persist to carry on in that state, they become psychiatric cases because "self" finally becomes frustrated.

A married Bible school student was apprehended by the police for sex exposure. When picked up for questioning, he resorted to the usual plea for leniency by stating that he did not recall he had committed the act of which he was accused. He pretended that he had a lapse of memory, or a blanking-out period, which justified the law in demanding that he have a psychiatric examination.

In the quietness of my consultation room he revealed what was in his heart: "I am a leader in the Bible school. It makes me feel important. When I am not active in the Lord's work I get depressed. I drive myself hard to build up my ego, hoping they will select me to be the leader in various activities. I don't solicit it, but I work for it. I am the leader of the group that has charge of the jail

136

services. I am also the leader of the group that holds youth meetings in the cities around here.

"I get depressed so easily, and my mood is down when I am not working for the Lord or when I do not put our program over. I drive myself hard in the Lord's work. The day I got caught I was depressed; I was low. Then I turned to my former practice [sex exposure], which I did before I was married and entered Bible school. I see now that I worked so hard for the Lord to keep my sin, which I had never overcome, hidden."

A pastor of a church said, "It seems I must be kept very busy to keep sex out of my thoughts. In pastoring a church I have too much idle time; then my mind turns to the wildest fantasies a man could imagine. I want to work for the Lord, but it must be something that requires all my thinking."

Perhaps you ask, Why does such an individual need to see a psychiatrist? Why doesn't he turn all his thoughts on the Lord? He turned to psychiatry because he was fearful of losing his mind. He realized that his thinking ability was impaired because sex fantasies were constantly being interjected into his thinking. He said, "I have the impulse to withdraw from the work at hand so I can indulge in my sex imaginations. When I go to my study, I ask my wife and child to be quiet so that I will not have any distractions [from his imaginations]. I feel I must give up my ministry. Satan harasses me with my past sex imaginations."

Again you may ask, Why doesn't he turn it all over to the Lord? That is exactly what he should do; however, that is not as simple as it may sound.

Need for Deliverance

Too often we Christians glibly answer a soul in trouble by parroting the oft-expressed phrase "Just pray about it." To many a sufferer this sounds as if we are sweeping the problem under the rug, so to speak. We need to realize that some Christians are so bound to self and Satan that they cannot pray. They can only think of their suffering, hopelessness and desperate need for deliverance.

My patient was much like the man our Lord met at the pool of Bethesda. This man had had an infirmity for 38 years. He could only plead his helpless state. Even though the Lord made him whole and made him walk to convince him he was well, the Lord deemed it necessary to give him some admonition regarding his past illness and his need to walk circumspectly so that he would not have a recurrence of his suffering: "Behold, thou art made whole: sin no more, lest a worse thing come unto thee" (John 5:14).

This man still had his will and his old personality; therefore, if he had not been warned of what caused his former infirmity, he would have been an easy prey for the same condition to return. Or as Jesus warned, "Lest a worse thing come unto thee."

The Lord knows how easy it is for an individual under the old influences to fall prey to Satan. And this case history shows how easy it is for Satan to entice the old self back into former habits when the patient is under the stimulation of the proper environment.

This pastor, like others in bondage to sexual imaginations, did not realize how subtly Satan works by suggesting sexual fantasies as a release from boredom. Over a period of years he had indulged himself by giving more and more time to sex fantasies until he found his thought processes so enmeshed in sexual imaginations that he could not continue his Bible study.

Not Overwork

He came for psychiatric help believing that he had overworked his mind, because he could no longer control his thinking. His wife and his parishioners were under the illusion that he "overworked doing the Lord's work." This was not overwork. It was part of the old self, which had not been reckoned crucified with Christ, and it gradually brought him into complete bondage to sin. Satan energized him to indulge in his former sexual imaginations.

Patients are often deluded into believing that overwork has caused their emotional illness. It is a case of self-desires being nurtured, not overworked. Self, which has not been reckoned crucified, is at the root of these problems.

Often Christians have joy after being released from some besetting satanic plague, but they forget to glorify God. They forget to commune with Him and to meditate on His Word. Therefore, in a moment of darkness, oppression and disappointment—when the mind is perplexed—the evil forces return with the former imaginations, the same evil spirits with the same lusts of sex. If the oppressions are of longer duration and deeper intensity, the range of fanciful sexual lusts increase in their scope. The Christian has failed to protect himself from the repeated onslaught of the evil forces by not keeping his thoughts on God.

Casting Down Imaginations

The Christian is commanded to cast down imaginations and to bring every thought into captivity to the obedience of Christ (II Cor. 10:5). He cannot do this in his fleshly nature. He can do this only as he keeps in mind his proper relationship with Christ. Every thought can be brought into captivity to Christ only as the Christian meditates on the Word and desires fellowship with Christ.

The pastor whom we have considered did not cast down imaginations. Eventually, he yielded to the increasing evil forces until he was in bondage to sexual fantasy. When he was in this latter state, he became fearful and sought psychiatric help. He really could not expect spiritual help from God because he was not bringing his thoughts into obedience to Christ.

The Christian who would work for the Lord must spend much time in fellowship with Him and in meditation on His Word.

You may conclude that this pastor had a sick mind—that his brain was diseased; therefore, he was a helpless victim of a diseased condition. A complete psychiatric study revealed no disease condition of his brain or of the physical nerves of his body. His problem was not in his mind but in his soul.

He was losing control of his realistic thinking because he willfully turned his thoughts to imaginations, the lust of the flesh. During the treatment he repeatedly brought accusations against Satan for putting sex thoughts into his mind. No doubt evil spirits were active in giving him sex thoughts when his mind was open for them. While he laid aside his "armour of God" to indulge in sin, they took advantage of their golden opportunity to bring him into bondage to sinful imaginations so his ministry would suffer.

Another patient who believed he was working for the Lord did not want to give up his besetting sin because "I might want to do it again." The patient was openly confessing that he intended to indulge in lust from time to time—whenever self desired to be indulgent. He had no intention of repenting; yet he recognized that he had a soul problem and wanted release from his worry.

His Christian convictions had led him to seek someone who could understand his problem in the light of Christianity. Had he been just a religious, unsaved individual, he would have considered his worry a problem of the mind, which needed psychiatric treatment for deliverance from suffering.

When the answer to his problem was being unfolded to him, he sensed his self-desires being frustrated. He wanted release from his worry without giving up the desires of self. He did not want to yield his self-nature "to the obedience of Christ."

The conflict of the flesh striving against the Spirit gave this patient psychiatric symptoms. He expected the Christian psychiatrist to remove these symptoms by prescribing a tranquilizer or, even better, by uttering some work of confirmation that sin is not always sin. A tranquilizer was not prescribed nor was he encouraged to indulge in his lust.

Too Much Religion

God calls men and women out of the world into His service. Satan, the great imitator of God, also calls men and women for his service. He activates the ego of the Christian who has not reckoned self as crucified, dead and buried with Christ to desire glory for itself, which can be attained through some religious endeavor.

Therefore, it is not unusual for some Christians to believe that a sermon on consecration is a call from God to give up their business and head for a pulpit or the foreign mission field.

Consecration to the Lord's service is truly commendable if the Lord gets the glory. Too often this sudden zeal to work for the Lord is not inspired by the Holy Spirit. The emotional self-pride of carnal Christians may drive them to do works in a related religious field.

In many cases the ego of the old nature drives the carnal Christian to sacrifice and suffer deprivations so he can give all of his time and strength to accomplish the work program he has set up for himself. On the surface, this zeal is quite impressive—and the worker believes he is in the Lord's work because the activity is in some religious field. The work, however, is not of the Lord's planning, even though the worker expects the Lord to bless it.

To be effective, all Christian work must depend on the power of God for its continuance. Furthermore, all Christian work, to be effective in the divine purpose, must be conceived by God. If we plan the work apart from God's guidance and then ask God to bless it, we need not expect Him to commit Himself to it. God's name can never be used by us as a rubber stamp to authorize work which is ours in conception. In such cases it is not done in His name but in our name.

We should always follow the admonition, "Commit thy works unto the Lord, and thy thoughts shall be established" (Prov. 16:3). When our thoughts are established by God, they will

143

center on bringing praise and glory to His name. Our work will then originate with God: "Working in you that which is wellpleasing in his sight, through Jesus Christ" (Heb. 13:21).

Christian workers who go in their own might and power, not in the Spirit of the Lord, eventually fail. They become frustrated and disappointed in their self-achievements—ending up as patients in need of psychiatric treatment.

It is the self which has not been reckoned crucified with Christ that gets frustrated. "Overwork" is the usual cover-up term used to disguise the truth. Non-Christian psychiatry says, "Overwork from too much religion." In one sense of the word, this diagnosis is true when we consider that these Christians are overworked by religious activities which glorify self, not by spiritual activities which glorify God.

Nervous Breakdowns and Works

So-called nervous breakdowns may occur in the "religious" workers in all fields of Christian work—Bible school students, seminary students, pastors and foreign missionaries.

The missionary who comes home from the foreign field suffering from mental and emotional illness has a sad story to tell—a story of frustration and defeat. But why the frustration? Defeated in what? By whom? Frustrated by his work. Defeated in his purpose. Overcome by self. Usually, before

144

the defeated missionary must turn his face homeward, he has become habituated to tranquilizers.

One missionary related her frustrations thus: "I just simply could not learn to love the natives. How does one learn to love them? We had them help with household duties so we could devote more time to working for the Lord. But when we found out they were stealing from us, I became angry and fired them. Then I had to do all the housework myself, besides help with the missionary work. I felt bitter toward them. It was hot, and I got tired and so irritable and exasperated that I lost control of myself.

"The bitterness gave me feelings which occupied my thoughts; my mind could not be free for the Holy Spirit. At first I always had my quiet time, but after a while I did not take time with the Lord. Angry thoughts pushed into my mind, and I could not think of Him. I cut out more and more of my time with the Lord so I would have more time for the work.

"I got so jittery I began to take tranquilizers. Over there I was able to get them without a prescription. I took more and more until I was taking so many I was out of my head. They finally had to bring me back here. What am I to do?"

Another missionary, instead of turning to the Lord as her frustrations increased, resorted to tranquilizers to dull the vexations of her work. "Things wear on me," said this missionary. "The native children bothered me when I couldn't make them understand. I couldn't get them to do things

145

in school without getting all upset. I worked harder and harder to get them to understand. Then these terrible migraine headaches began. At first tranquilizers helped some, but finally I had to take too many to do any good. Then I went to a psychiatrist.

"I knew the psychiatrist wasn't a Christian, because when I told him I couldn't read my Bible anymore, he retorted, 'If you just keep your mind off yourself you'll be all right.' But he gave me no suggestions about how to keep my mind off myself or how to keep from getting all upset until I hurt inside."

Through Christian psychotherapy this patient learned that her own driving effort would not accomplish the work the Lord had given her to do—that she needed to turn from carnal striving to rest in the Lord and find her strength in Him.

Excerpts from the history of a missionary who had to be brought back to the homeland for psychiatric treatment reveal some interesting facts about the struggle with carnality that occurs when the missionary goes to the field for his own purpose and in his own power: "I have had several series of electric shock treatments since I left the field. When I recovered sufficiently to go home after each series of shock treatments, I received calls to preach from the churches that supported me.

"I got terribly tense about the speaking engagements, but still I always hoped God would use me mightily. Then, while I was speaking, I would have

146

an exhilarated feeling come over me. It over-powered me, and something seemed to say to me, 'Now the Lord is using you mightily.' I would get so excited I could not control myself. In a short time I had maniacal outbursts and had to be subdued by force. I resisted the restraint. In my mental confusion I thought those who were re-straining me were hindering my work. I wanted to preach."

Just what was it that overpowered the patient? He himself said it was a feeling—"an exhilarated feeling." Who told him that the Lord was using him mightily? He said that it was "something" that "seemed" to say the Lord was using him. That "something" was his wish that the Lord would use him mightily, and in his confusion and illusion his self-life, which he had not reckoned as crucified, strove to make the wish reality.

During one of the hours of psychotherapy the patient said, "If I preached only once on Sunday, the thought that God was using me mightily would take hold of me and make me sick for several days. Even if I did not go out of control, I still was on the verge of a maniacal outburst. I finally refrained from preaching, but I desire fellowship with Christians so I go to church. Invariably I am invited to teach a Sunday school class. Even there I have trouble, but it does not get me down. What can I do with my life? I have not had any special training. I feel defeated and depressed because I know I cannot go back to the foreign field."

This patient's rather lengthy psychiatric history further reveals his motive for going to the foreign mission field: "My brothers are financially successful businessmen, and I knew I could not compete with them. So I decided to make a success in an entirely different vocation and chose the foreign mission field."

He did not say that the Lord had called him to the mission field but that he had made the choice. It was evident from his history that he went in the carnal confidence of proving to his family that he could make a name for himself.

Remember, it was not the spirit that had the nervous breakdown. It was the soul that had the confusion, delusion, maniacal outbursts, and nervous breakdown. His eye was not on the Lord but on his ego—the "I" that had not been reckoned crucified with Christ.

Concluding Facts About Works

I have cited but a few cases of missionaries who have been returned to the homeland because of mental and emotional problems, but they will suffice to shed further light on facts concerning works for the Lord.

So-called works for the Lord do not cure mental and emotional problems. Without the love of God in our hearts, works are unprofitable. Religious work for self-glory is frustrating. Satan has free access to the old self when the worker achieves self-glory. The worker who goes to the mission field in carnal confidence, not inspired by the Holy Spirit, is powerless against the wiles of the Devil. The carnal Christian is concerned about working for the Lord. The spiritual Christian finds joy in serving the Lord because he follows the Lord's blueprint.

Chapter 10

Where Can We Go?

"Where can I find a Christian psychiatrist?" I find this question in multitudes of letters. The letters state the question like this: "Do you know of a Christian psychiatrist in my city, area, or state who will deal with my emotional problems from the Christian viewpoint? I am a Christian and I do not want to go to a non-Christian with my problems."

Some will ask, Why must the counselor be a Christian? Why is this so important? Do not all psychiatrists have the same basic academic training? Why make a distinction for the Christian with emotional problems? Do Christians have different problems?

Yes! The born-again Christian is an enigma to the non-Christian counselor. The Spirit of Christ within cannot be comprehended by the five natural senses. This is a mysterious puzzle to the unsaved, natural man. The things of God are "foolishness unto him: neither can he know them, because they are spiritually discerned" (I Cor. 2:14).

A non-Christian psychiatrist, when asked to address a seminar of deans of Christian Bible

150

schools, said, "I do not see any need to have an organization of deans just for Christian Bible colleges. Why not include the deans of all schools of higher learning?" This scholarly, non-Christian psychiatrist was expressing his lack of spiritual comprehension of soul problems of the Christian.

The following statements and excerpts from letters my patients have written, giving their personal experiences and reactions in seeking psychiatric help, should guide and encourage others in similar situations:

"I hated to tell non-Christians my sins and problems. It seemed to dishonor God."

"The psychiatrist at the mental hygiene clinic was disinterested in my spiritual problems. He was bored and annoyed. He made me feel loathsome."

"My husband and I cooperated fully with the doctors, but recovery was uncertain. I realized there was a deficiency in their therapy, for I was a saved person and there was no mention of spiritual help or need. I longed and sought for spiritual help."

"My doctor sent me to a psychiatrist. I felt very strongly I should not be in the psychiatrist's office, as I sensed he was not a Christian. I wondered how he could possibly understand the working of the mind of a born-again Christian."

"When I went to the other psychiatrist, I was fighting two battles. I knew I should take the medicine [psychotherapy], but I was afraid of what it might do to my Christianity."

"I sought help from two psychiatrists while in nurses' training. They had me believing my problem stemmed from childhood fears. I knew I had had many and that this was part of it. But they failed to see the place Satan fills in this pattern."

"When they saw me read my Bible on the psychiatric ward, they forbade me to visit with other patients."

"When we disagreed in spiritual matters, I doubted the psychiatrist in other matters."

"We persuaded my brother [a Christian] to go to a Christian hospital. He felt so hopeful after he heard it was run by a church organization that he opened up and talked about his religious conflicts, quoting Scripture. During the first interview the psychiatrist offered my brother a cigarette. He insisted that my brother was a religious fanatic. In later interviews he stopped my brother whenever he made any reference to his religious conflicts."

"I was trapped into believing the falsehood that my problems were primarily emotional, not spiritual. I was enticed by the psychiatrist's philosophy and his numerous religious activities. It was hard for me to believe a rank modernist and liberal could be so religiously active. He was a Sunday school teacher and sponsor of a teenage class of young people in the largest church of that city. God pity those young people! I learned my lesson too late. I looked at his works, not his fruit, and was taken in."

"Dr. _____ set Christ aside and instead dealt with my fleshly problems. He kept pointing out these problems as human and, therefore, natural. He tried to make me believe I could not believe everything I read in the Bible. He said that you can prove anything by the Bible."

"I believe I am a spiritual Christian. It is necessary that I see someone who is well acquainted with the Lord."

"How I long to have someone to talk to that understands my spiritual problem."

"Psychiatry opened all my problems to me. It gave me no answers. I have spent thousands of dollars, but that money went right down the drain. I do not feel delivered and restored. Now I feel hopeless! Now, where to go."

"I cannot leave things in the Lord's hands. I have been too psychological the past five years. I have lost the simplicity of faith that I had when I was first saved. This all came about when I felt the need of help. Believing it was a psychological problem, I turned to psychological sources—books, magazines and counselors—which got me to think psychologically."

"I went to a family counseling service for help. A lady advised me to adjust to the world through clubs, learn to live with people, and do things with people. She thought I lived in a world of unreality because I did not go to worldly things such as clubs, movies and dances. She thought I was a schizophrenic because I could not live as the rest of the world. She said I had better go to a psychiatrist. I told all this to a psychiatrist. I could tell he was not a Christian. He suggested I go to an

153

institution for six months. I do not think I am a schizophrenic, but it bothers me to be told I am one."

These are not isolated cases. Christian patients often tell me they are afraid to talk to their doctors about spiritual problems. They are afraid the doctors, not being Christians, will interpret their separated lives and their unfamiliar statements as being fanaticism and delusions and will want to send them to a psychiatrist or a mental institution. This is one of the most frequent reasons Christians with emotional problems defer seeking help while they can still be helped.

A frightened, nervous Christian wrote: "You see, my problem is whether or not I believe in God. This has been going on for some years now. I thought I believed but now I do not know. I am so confused, and I have such a tight feeling in my throat and chest. What if it would strangle me and I am not sure I believe? What if it would kill me and I am not sure I am saved? I have been to so many doctors. The last one scared me and added to my misery. He advised shock treatment without examining me and did not talk to me over 15 minutes. I have determined that I will never go to another non-Christian psychiatrist. They have only added to my misery. Where can I go? Where can I find a Christian psychiatrist?"

Another nervous Christian wrote: "I went to five psychiatrists but it did not seem to me that we could agree on spiritual matters, so they were not able to help me. I am a Christian. Can you

154

recommend a Christian psychiatrist in my area? Where can I find a real Christian psychiatrist? They say they are Christians, but they are not born again."

Non-Christian Psychiatry, Carnal Christians, the Unsaved

The carnal Christian, bound to self and tied to this world, does not have any qualms or reactions in counseling with a non-Christian psychiatrist. Being more worldly oriented, he is naturally inclined to seek help from those who help him to make an adjustment to the world. He does not have sufficient spiritual conviction to sense his spiritual need. His emotional suffering draws him away from God, for when he suffers emotionally he turns to the world for a panacea. This can vary anywhere from mental diversions to sedatives, tranquilizers, electric shock and various types of brain surgery.

The non-Christian patient has no problem at all in this area and naturally does not have any unfavorable reaction in consulting a non-Christian psychiatrist. Why should he? Both he and the unsaved psychiatrist are natural-born citizens of this world under Satan's domain. They have one purpose in life—to adjust to this world.

Salvation Through Affliction

I have not found it unusual, however, for a man of the world seeking psychiatric help to cry

155

out that he is helpless—that he has tried everything the world has to offer. At such times, at the end of himself, he intuitively says he has prayed to God (whatever that means to him) and asked God to help him. This is without doubt the door that the Holy Spirit opens to the unsaved. The Spirit guides and directs the distressed soul to someone who will lead him to Christ. He is indeed fortunate when he happens to contact a Christian counselor at such a time.

I believe such patients to be the souls whom the Holy Spirit has prepared through affliction to seek the face of God through the shed blood of Jesus Christ on Calvary and find everlasting life in Christ. These are the ones who, when they are saved, will rejoice with the psalmist in saying, "It is good for me that I have been afflicted; that I might learn thy statutes" (Ps. 119:71).

When Psychiatrists Are Nominal Christians

One psychiatrist confided to the writer, "I am a Christian but I do not use the Christian approach in my office practice. I just do not go that far."

Psychiatrists who are nominal Christians (in name only) are a real problem to Christian patients seeking a Christian psychiatrist. These nominal Christians are actually non-Christians.

Most non-Christian psychiatrists, in their own way of thinking, believe they are Christians because they live in a civilized, literate country. Furthermore, many conform to the conventional

156

morals and perhaps even the religious ethics of some church group.

A non-Christian psychiatrist does not necessarily intend to be deceptive. His natural senses cannot discern the meaning of being "born again." He understands Christianity only as he perceives religion through his natural senses.

One patient drew this conclusion after being to a so-called Christian psychiatrist for several interviews: "I was wanting to be charitable to him—he may be saved—but he does not show evidence that he loves the Lord. He kept the Lord at arm's length all through the treatment."

Searching for a Christian Psychiatrist

One patient wrote: "We consulted a psychiatrist who had been recommended by a Christian psychologist. We asked the psychiatrist if he were a Christian. His reply was, 'I am a church member [he named the denomination]. That should answer your question.'

"When we brought up a question about spiritual problems, the psychiatrist would say, 'We will let your pastor deal with your religious problems.' We thought this was a suggestion that we should not expect him to deal with spiritual problems. Whenever any reference was made to Christianity he reminded us, 'You can take that up with your pastor. That is a theological problem.' "

What is the Christian with emotional problems to do if he has been referred to a non-Christian

157

psychiatrist by a pastor? What about his spiritual problem? To whom can he go? He should seek a pastor who preaches the gospel of the Lord Jesus Christ according to the Bible. After all, he may be obliged to consult a Christian pastor if he cannot find a Christian psychiatrist.

Christian Patients and Non-Christian Psychiatrists

How well the Christian patient can adjust to the non-Christian psychiatrist depends very much on the spiritual state of the patient. Is the Christian patient able to communicate with the non-Christian psychiatrist? In psychiatric language we would say, "Can they establish a rapport?"

One Christian patient said, "I lost confidence in the psychiatrist before beginning treatment with him, even though he was recommended by a Christian organization. He indicated that the bone to be set in a Christian or non-Christian required the same technical ability. He said that basically a Christian would set the bone in the same manner as a non-Christian. Then he added that in like manner a non-Christian and Christian would receive the same psychotherapy. I was afraid to say what was on my mind during therapy for fear we would get into an argument."

The same Christian patient sought another psychiatrist recommended to her in another state, who had what seemed creditable Christian cre-dentials: "I asked him point-blank what his relationship was with the Lord. He replied, 'I am a

158

member of the church and served in Africa under the church mission board.'

"To me it seemed everything of a spiritual nature was excluded until catharsis was complete and adjustment was under way. His attitude seemed to be: 'Now, let's not go too far with this sort of thing.' I could not discuss my problem freely. I was to leave my Christian principles as if I were odd for being a Bible-believing Christian."

The Christian patient who presents his problem to the non-Christian psychiatrist must, of course, reveal his entire problem. He cannot give him only what he thinks will not stir up the Christian problems—as if he decided beforehand to present to the unsaved psychiatrist only the non-Christian problems.

One Christian desperately in need of help said, "I had no place to turn so I decided to go through with the treatment. I tried to give him what I thought he would accept, but I was careful not to hint to my Christian needs. I guess it was the tranquilizers he gave me that helped me endure the sessions with him. Near the end of each session he stressed my need for further treatment. He had me believing that I was sicker than I really was. He kept saying that you need to have faith in yourself, then you will have faith in God. But I knew that having faith in self is not going to give me faith in God. I knew he had no knowledge of faith in God. How could he help me?"

A minister wrote: "I found one doctor who was a Christian everywhere but in his practice. He always wanted to put my religious views aside. I felt he was afraid God would get some credit for delivering me, whereas he wanted all the credit for curing me."

Do you dare yield your mind and heart to the non-Christian psychiatrist? The following letter illustrates the kind of frustration that comes to the Christian who seeks counsel from a non-Christian psychiatrist:

"The doctor kept me in his office one hour trying to tell me my belief was too strict. He also said the Bible is not true in many places. He said I should not believe that people who are not Christians cannot go to heaven. I quoted scripture after scripture but he was willfully blind. I want to talk to someone who knows the workings of the mind and who, at the same time, is a true Christian."

Satanic Oppressions

The following is a confession and at the same time a testimony: "I am struggling almost constantly to hang onto my sanity. Prayer and Bible reading are the only things that keep me going. I have prayed for guidance and the Lord is surely standing by me. But is life supposed to be such a struggle?"

Christians are reading, hearing and seeing so much about psychology today that unless they keep their eyes on the Lord, they will become too introspective. This Christian was tormented with

160

fear of losing her mind and was tempted to reach out for psychiatric help. Yet, from her testimony, she was using the best psychotherapy available for a Christian. This was not a psychiatric problem—a problem of the mind; it was a spiritual struggle—oppression by Satan.

She did not seem to recognize the subtleties of Satan, who was attacking her thinking, trying to introduce doubts of her sanity. Being surrounded by the psychiatric atmosphere of this era, she was letting some of Satan's psychology enter her thinking, starting the little seed of doubt as to her sanity.

We must remember that Satan can communicate with his own in this world through his modern psychology, but he is also attempting to communicate with Christians. He is waging a battle to control the minds of Christians by making them think they are out of step with this world; therefore, not truly sane. For consolation we turn once again to the Bible, where we read that Christ gave Himself for us to purify unto Himself a peculiar people zealous to please Him—which makes us Christians maladjusted to this world.

A minister who loved the Lord was tormented with the thought that he must be suffering from a psychiatric condition. He said, "I have depressed periods when I doubt my salvation. Am I depending on the blood of Christ or is it self? I wake up at night in a cold sweat, wondering if I am saved. Then my past sins and wickedness come before my mind. What if I should die before morning? What if my religion is all mental and not of the heart? The thing that is so frightening when I am in a depression is that God seems so far away. Doubts come in. If I am wrong about one thing, I could be wrong about other things as well. If I do not trust the Lord, I am a false preacher misleading the people. Maybe I let newspapers and TV hinder my meditation. When I pray I have to ask, Am I praying to myself or in daydreams? I am sure I have a mental defect of some kind. If it continues to increase, I am sure I will end up in a psychotic condition. I admit I have been doing too much introspecting."

This minister gave up his church and resigned himself to the false idea that he was a psychiatric patient in need of mind treatment. Yet there was no disease of his mind, either inherited or self-induced. As he aired his problem he was able to see that Satan played the major role in his suffering, for as he said later, "I got to dwelling on my doubts instead of claiming the promises for my salvation and the forgiveness of my sins. I blame myself, really, in that I had too much interest in psychiatry. I saw my symptoms in the light of modern psychiatry. The psychological treatment of my symptoms made me more psychology-minded than Christ-minded. The tranquilizers prescribed by the doctors helped to depress me. The depression left me as I was able to yield my mind fully to the Lord. I never saw this as a satanic oppression. I guess I had to learn it to make me a better minister in the Lord's service."

162

Psychiatrists Differ From Their Colleagues in Medicine

As a physician, the psychiatrist has much in common with his colleagues in other branches of medicine. However, his position is unique. Whether the patient is a clergyman or an agnostic, the surgeon removes the inflamed appendix. Whether his patient is a saint or a sinner, the orthopedic surgeon treats the fracture by the same scientific technique. Not so the psychiatrist. He is a scientist, but in his practice he must frequently relinquish the role of scientist.

For instance, his patient may present a sense of guilt. He must decide if the guilt is real or neurotic. Does the patient need psychotherapy for a neurosis, or does he need to understand Christ's atonement for sin? Therapy must be directed toward understanding the underlying causes.

In the process of evaluating the problem, he may attempt to play a neutral role by appearing abstract, keeping aloof and not expressing his attitude toward guilt or sin. One patient expressed his feeling toward a seemingly neutral interview he endured: "He [the psychiatrist] sat there like a sphinx, pretending to know more than he was letting on. But I knew what he thought."

In the process of psychotherapy, a relationship is established in which, either by spoken word or by nonverbal cues, the psychiatrist reveals his attitude either for or against what the patient says. There is no neutral interview in a psychiatrist's office. Do not let any non-Christian counselor beguile you into believing that during the process of psychotherapy he will—or even can—remain neutral to your Christian and moral views.

Analyzing the Psychiatrist's Testimony

Even though the Christian patient may be fortunate enough to stumble onto a Christian psychiatrist, he still faces a problem. Is the psychiatrist really born again? Or does he bear the label of Christian because of his religious organizational affiliations? And most important—does he practice Christian psychotherapy in his office practice, or is he afraid of the criticism from his professional colleagues?

The Christian patient must make the initial approach to determine not only the psychiatrist's academic qualifications but also where he stands with Christ. Does he love the Lord? Does the love of God shine forth? This cannot be hidden from a spiritual Christian patient.

A Christian contacted a psychiatrist recommended to her by a reliable Christian organization. She said, "I finally worked up courage to ask Dr. _____ if he were born again. He was a little taken aback and replied that he was a religious person and would do his professional best. I had my doubts about his Christianity. Then I asked, 'How do you feel about the importance of Christ's death and shed blood on the cross in relation to salvation?' He said that he felt it was different for different people and that I was trying to make it a blanket thing for all people. I could not get him to

164

state his personal relationship to the Lord. I concluded he had none. That settled it for me. I did not take my husband to him because my husband is a worldly Christian and I was afraid that he would be encouraged to continue in his present state."

Another Christian patient who probed for a definite Christian testimony from her psychiatrist received this answer: "I could spend all day talking religion with you, yet not get at your problems." Needless to say, this patient did not go any further with her interview. She had psychological problems, but they could not have been dealt with without considering her Christian way of life.

The carnal Christian analyzes his psychiatrist with a different objective. He is not as much concerned about his counselor's salvation as he is that the psychiatrist agrees with his doctrine, creed and ideologies of his denomination.

Seeking Confirmation

Seeking a Christian psychiatrist, in the minds of some patients, does not necessarily always mean a psychiatrist who is born again. They may be seeking someone to agree with them in their way of life. Their self-nature is so unyielding it interferes with any attempt to counsel them. They are not seeking advice (counseling) for a problem, but a counselor who will agree with their ego desires.

When so-called Christian patients seek a Christian psychiatrist, they may be seeking someone to reinterpret the Bible. For example: "Does

165

the Book [instead of saying 'Bible') always mean what it says about divorce? I want a divorce. I cannot tolerate my husband any longer. My love life with a married man is so perfect, so right, I cannot even feel ashamed of it."

Interpreting the Bible to please this patient's illicit desires would not have been the answer to her problem.

Conclusion

The Christian with emotional problems must first understand the meaning of the finished work of Christ. He must see his identity with Christ, who bore his sins on the cross. He must reckon himself crucified, dead and buried with Christ. Because the Christian has died with Christ, his life is hid with Christ in God (Col. 3:3).

"Therefore if any man be in Christ, he is a new creature: old things are passed away; behold, all things are become new" (II Cor. 5:17).

If the Christian has not reckoned self crucified, and if his emotional problems—such as doubt, anxiety, worry and fear—are so deeply rooted that his pastor or counselors are unable to get at the root of his suffering, he should seek professional help. He should not continue to hassle with the problems until he is overcome by the forces of Satan.

In the final analysis, the answer will be the same as it has been for many, many centuries: "Jesus Christ the same yesterday, and to day, and for ever" (Heb. 13:8).

166

Chapter 11

Victorious Living

by Theodore H. Epp

God has made provision that we do not have to sin. This is not to say that our old nature has been eradicated, nor is it to say that we will not sin. But it is to say that through the death of Christ, God has made provision that we do not have to sin.

The Book of Romans contains many basic doctrinal statements concerning what God has done for us. In this book, particularly in chapter 6, we are also told how we can attain a life that will be pleasing in the sight of God.

The first five chapters in the Book of Romans tell of sin, its consequences, how Jesus paid its penalty, and the way to salvation. Chapters 6-8 deal with the subject of sin in the believer's life after he has been saved. This has to do with the dominion of sin in the believer's life.

The difference between the words "sin" and "sins" needs to be clearly understood. "Sin" refers to the powerful principle of sin that lies in the old nature, or the old man. It is this principle or nature that enslaves us and produces "sins," which are the

167

acts of the sinful nature. We commit acts of sin because we have a sin nature. At the cross, God not only dealt with the acts of sin, but He also brought judgment on our sin nature.

The powerful sin nature wants to continuously enslave a person, even after he has received Jesus Christ as Saviour. The question each believer must answer is, Am I going to continue to stumble because of the sin nature, or am I going to be a positive conqueror in Christ? Do you long to be set free from the enslavement of sin? As a believer, the Apostle Paul longed to be free from sin's dominion, but he had to admit, "I have the will but not the power to do what is right. Indeed, I do not do the good things that I want to do, but I do practice the evil things that I do not want to do. . . . Wretched man that I am! Who can save me from this deadly lower nature?" (Rom. 7:18,19,24,*Wms.*). These words express Paul's frustration in the Christian life before he came to realize how he could be victorious over sin.

Whereas Romans 5 tells us what we have *through* Christ because of His death, chapters 6-8 tell us what we have *in* Christ because of His life. The believer can live victoriously because of his union with the living Christ. Christ fully met all the requirements for our redemption when He paid for our sins. When we received Him as Saviour, we became children of God and were delivered from condemnation. But this is not all that Christ has provided. He has also provided what is needed to give us complete victory in this life.

168

At the conclusion of Romans 5, the Apostle Paul said, "But where sin abounded, grace did much more abound: That as sin hath reigned unto death, even so might grace reign through righteousness unto eternal life by Jesus Christ our Lord" (vv. 20,21). In Romans 6:1, Paul raised the question, "What shall we say then? Shall we continue in sin, that grace may abound?" Notice that Paul was talking about "sin," which is the sin nature we inherited from Adam. Because grace is more evident where sin exists, Paul was asking his readers if they thought they should continue to live under the domination of the old nature in order that the grace of God might be more evident. Paul was not talking about the sinner's relationship to acts of sin but about his relationship to the nature of sin. The believer has no right to live under the control of the old nature—living the way he pleases in accordance to the old self-life.

Not Sinless Perfection

There is an important distinction to be made between sinless perfection and what the Bible means by the words "perfect" and "perfection." Sinless perfection is the teaching that a believer can reach a point in this life where he can be sure that he will never sin again. The Apostle John referred to those who make such a claim when he wrote: "If we say that we have no sin, we deceive ourselves, and the truth is not in us" (I John 1:8). The person who claims his sin nature has been

169

eradicated only deceives himself, because it is not true. This is what those do who know they are sinners but who believe that after one receives Jesus Christ as Saviour, he reaches a point where he no longer commits sins. On the other hand, John said that "if we say that we have not sinned, we make him a liar, and his word is not in us" (v. 10). If we say that we have never sinned, we make God a liar. The Scriptures make it abundantly clear in such verses as Romans 3:23 that "all have sinned, and come short of the glory of God." To deny such a truth is to call God a liar.

When the Bible uses "perfect" or "perfection" in referring to the believer's walk, it refers to spiritual maturity. Hebrews 6:1 says, "Therefore leaving the principles of the doctrine of Christ, let us go on unto perfection." This does not refer to sinless perfection but to spiritual maturity. Sinless perfection is only self-deception, but spiritual maturity is to be the goal of every Christian. Spiritual maturity is the result of our living in fellowship with the Lord and of our refusing to practice sin even though we are living in the presence of sin. We become spiritually mature as we refuse to allow the sin nature to overpower us and to control our lives. Believers become spiritually mature as they apply God's method of control over the sin nature which produces sins in their lives. It is possible for the mature believer to sin, but he knows he does not have to sin because its power over him has been broken.

Dead to Sin

Having asked, "Shall we continue in sin, that grace may abound?" Paul emphatically answered, "God forbid. How shall we that are dead to sin, live any longer therein?" (v. 2). The phrase "we that are dead to sin" is, literally, "we who have died to sin." The verb is in the past tense, emphasizing that the believer's death to sin took place in the past. It was made effective in the person when he received Jesus Christ as his Saviour, for at that very moment he died to the principle of sin and the grace of God triumphed.

Notice that sin (the old nature) did not die, but we died to it. Victory over the domination of the sin nature is possible only as we have the right attitude toward our relationship to the sin nature. It is not so much our attitude toward sins—the fruit of the sin nature—as it is toward sin—the sin nature itself. The believer's relationship to the sin nature is that he has died to it and has been made alive unto God.

The Apostle Paul then asked, "Know ye not, that so many of us as were baptized into Jesus Christ were baptized into his death?" (v. 3). Paul intimated that some believers either had forgotten or had never known that they had been baptized into the death of Jesus Christ. There was ignorance on the part of many about this crucial truth. Provisions for a perfect (spiritually mature) life are plentiful, but defeat lies largely in our ignorance of what has been provided for us. The power for

171

victorious Christian living does not result from our imitating Christ but from our appropriating by faith the provisions He has made for us.

It is important that we know that the Christian life is Christ's life in the believer. Christ came to put away sin by the sacrifice of Himself; now we are to put down sin by the surrender of ourselves to the principles of this new life.

In Romans 5:10 Paul said, "For if, when we were enemies, we were reconciled to God by the death of his Son, much more, being reconciled, we shall be saved by his life." In order for us to be reconciled to God it was necessary for Christ to die for us. This salvation involves more than just being saved from the guilt of sin. It also involves being saved from the power of sin. Having received Jesus Christ as Saviour, who reconciles us to God, Paul said, "We shall be saved by his life." The Christian life is properly lived as we, by active faith, let Jesus Christ live His life in us.

Death, Burial and Resurrection

Having reminded the believers that those who were baptized into Jesus Christ were baptized into His death, Paul said, "Therefore we are buried with him by baptism into death: that like as Christ was raised up from the dead by the glory of the Father, even so we also should walk in newness of life" (6:4). The believer's position in Christ's death, burial and resurrection is pictured by baptism. Baptism is not a means of salvation; it is a symbol

172

of what was accomplished in salvation. Only the death of Christ could pay the penalty for sin; therefore, we can have salvation only by receiving Him as our Saviour (I John 2:2; John 1:12).

Baptism is an expression of our faith in Christ and is a symbol of what took place at the time of salvation. The believer is a partaker in the death, burial and resurrection of Jesus Christ. Because we died with Christ and were buried with Him, the sin nature no longer has control over our lives. Just as Christ rose from the dead, we also have been raised to walk in newness of life. We are partakers of His divine life, and we are to walk in the strength and power of His life. It is not that He has renewed our old life, but rather, having died with Him, we now have His life within us. Because Christ lives in us, we live in a completely new spiritual realm.

This new spiritual realm is referred to in Colossians 1:13, which says the Father "hath delivered us from the power of darkness, and hath translated us into the kingdom of his dear Son." Because of our decision to receive Christ as Saviour, we have been taken from the sphere where sin has absolute dominion and have been placed into a new sphere where Christ has absolute dominion. Because we have received Christ as Saviour, the rights that sin previously had to dominate us have all been canceled. Because Christ is our new Master, we now have a new nature and can denounce and defy the old nature.

Freedom from the old nature, through death to the old nature, is also seen in verse 7 of Romans 6:

173

"For he that is dead [literally, "has died"] is freed from sin." This does not mean that such a person will never sin again, but it does mean that he is freed from the claims of sin—from its power and slavery. The old nature no longer has any right to control the person who has received Christ as Saviour and, as a result, has died to sin. Such a person has passed from death to life and has no obligations to the old nature.

Even though it is wonderful to know these truths, they are just information unless they are applied to our lives. This is where Romans 6:11 becomes very important: "Likewise reckon ye also yourselves to be dead indeed unto sin, but alive unto God through Jesus Christ our Lord." The knowledge we now possess is to become the basis for a decisive action. Thus the Apostle Paul said, "Reckon ye." The word "reckon" means "to take into account" or "to consider as true, calculate." We are to take into account what God really means when He says that we have died to sin and are alive unto Him. We need to consider it as true, *because it is true* if we have received Christ as our Saviour.

A Twofold Work

Our being dead to sin and living unto God has to do with our identification with Christ's death. There are two aspects of the cross that we should never forget. First, Christ died *for* sin. This was His substitutionary death for us. By His death on the cross, He became "the propitiation [satisfaction]

174

for our sins: and not for our's only, but also for the sins of the whole world" (I John 2:2). Christ paid for our sins through the shedding of His own blood. Hebrews 9:22 tells us that "without shedding of blood is no remission [forgiveness]."

Second, we died with Him *to* sin. This truth is emphasized in Galatians 2:20: "I am crucified [literally, "have been crucified"] with Christ: nevertheless I live; yet not I, but Christ liveth in me: and the life which I now live in the flesh I live by the faith of the Son of God, who loved me, and gave himself for me." Once a person places his faith in Jesus Christ as his Saviour, he becomes a partaker in Christ's crucifixion so it can be said that he has been crucified with Christ. It is a past act that has been completed but the effects of it continue.

The first aspect of the cross—Christ's death for sin—has to do with the penalty for sin. The second aspect of the cross—our death with Christ to sin—has to do with the power of sin. Because we have died to sin, it no longer has power over us. Not only has its penalty been paid by Christ's death for sin, but its power has also been broken because in Christ we died to sin.

When Christ died on the cross, He broke Satan's power to hold people in slavery to sin. Speaking of Christ, Hebrews 2:14 says, "Forasmuch then as the children are partakers of flesh and blood, he also himself likewise took part of the same; that through death he might destroy him that had the power of death, that is, the

175

devil." The word "destroy" in this verse means "to render inoperative." Christ broke Satan's power of operation. Satan was not destroyed as a person, but his power was destroyed. If you have received Christ as your Saviour, Satan has no right to you anymore. His power has been broken and you do not need to yield to him. How do we make this real in our lives? By faith—by reckoning these things to be true because they are true. As we take God at His word, we will experience the victory that He has made possible. Satan is not dead and sin is not dead. But by our death, burial and resurrection with Christ, we have been transferred to a new realm—we have been delivered from the power of darkness and have been translated into the kingdom of His dear Son (Col. 1:13).

How to Overcome

When you learn how to overcome sin, it will revolutionize your entire life. There are four words that present the crucial steps to overcoming sin. Three of these words are found in Romans 6 and the other is found in Romans 8. The words are *know*, *reckon*, *yield* and *walk*.

What we need to *know* is in Romans 6:6: "Knowing this, that our old man is crucified with him, that the body of sin might be destroyed, that henceforth we should not serve sin." The crucifixion referred to in this verse is a past crucifixion because it took place at the cross. The

176

phrase "is crucified" should literally read, "was crucified."

The word "destroyed" in Romans 6:6 is the same word used regarding Satan in Hebrews 2:14. There we saw that the word means "to render inoperative" and has to do with breaking Satan's power. So also, Romans 6:6 teaches that the power of sin to enslave us has been broken or made inactive as far as the believer is concerned. The reason for this is given in verse 7: "For he that is dead is freed from sin."

Unless we know what is taught in Romans 6 about the believer's having died to sin, we will not be able to live the victorious Christian life as God intends. But it is even more than knowing the information involved; we must ask God to enable us to spiritually understand these truths. As the Apostle Paul prayed for the Ephesians, we need to pray that the eyes of our understanding will be enlightened concerning these truths. As we grow in our understanding of what it means for the old man to be crucified, we will experience greater victory and freedom in the Christian life. The Christian need not yield to the pull of sin in his life. In Christ, the believer has died to sin; and a dead person does not respond to the forces about him, no matter how strong they are.

In addition to knowing that we have died to the old nature, we need to *reckon* it so—consider it true because it is true. Romans 6:11 tells us, "Likewise reckon ye also yourselves to be dead indeed unto sin, but alive unto God through Jesus

177

Christ our Lord." The word translated "reckon" is sometimes translated "impute," which means "to put on account." Because we have received Christ as Saviour, God has imputed to our account the fact that we have died to sin. Our responsibility now is to count on this fact, or reckon it to be so.

Have you learned to say No to the old nature? Do you realize that all that you are and have belongs to God? Romans 6:11 involves a twofold reckoning. We are to reckon ourselves to be dead unto sin and alive unto God through Jesus Christ our Lord. To say only that the believer has died to sin is to stop short of stating the entire truth. The believer is one who is also living unto God. Realizing the wonderful truth that the power of sin has been broken, we are now to live unto God by giving Him all that we are and have.

Because the believer has died to sin, Paul exhorted, "Let not sin therefore reign in your mortal body, that ye should obey it in the lusts thereof" (v. 12). The believer has died to the sin nature, and he does not need to let sin be king in his life. Say No to the temptation, and trust the Holy Spirit to make your No effective.

Knowing that we have died to sin, and reckoning it to be true, we need to *yield* to God. "Neither yield ye your members as instruments of unrighteousness unto sin: but yield yourselves unto God, as those that are alive from the dead, and your members as instruments of righteousness unto God" (v. 13). In this case, the word "yield" means "present." The believer is to present himself to

God as one who is alive from the dead, and he is to present his members as instruments of righteousness unto God. The word translated "yield" in Romans 6:13 is the same word translated "present" in Romans 12:1: "I beseech you therefore, brethren, by the mercies of God, that ye present your bodies a living sacrifice, holy, acceptable unto God, which is your reasonable service." The believer is to refuse to yield to sin; but he is to yield, or present, all that he is and has to God. Paul reminded the Roman Christians, "Know ye not, that to whom ye yield yourselves servants to obey, his servants ye are to whom ye obey; whether of sin unto death, or of obedience unto righteousness?" (6:16).

Notice, the believer must decide to whom he will yield. He has the power to say No and he has the power to say Yes. We must know what we have in Christ, reckon it to be so, refuse to yield to sin, and yield ourselves to God. As Christians, we belong to God. First Corinthians 6:19,20 says, "What? know ye not that your body is the temple of the Holy Ghost which is in you, which ye have of God, and ye are not your own? For ye are bought with a price: therefore glorify God in your body, and in your spirit, which are God's." Because we totally belong to Him, we should present all that we are and have to Him. Nothing is ours alone. Our need is to present ourselves to God with no reservations. Then we are commanded in Romans 12:2: "Be not conformed to this world: but be ye transformed by the renewing of your

179

mind, that ye may prove what is that good, and acceptable, and perfect, will of God."

The fourth word, which sums up what the believer must do if he is to have a victorious Christian life, is *walk*. Romans 8:4 says, "That the righteousness of the law might be fulfilled in us, who walk not after the flesh, but after the Spirit." Believers are not to walk according to the sin nature but according to the leading of the indwelling Holy Spirit. The believer is to know, reckon, yield and walk.

How to Appropriate

It is not enough to know these truths; they must be applied to our lives if we are going to have victory over sin as God intends us to have. We need to appropriate what Christ has accomplished for us and live accordingly.

The principle of appropriation is seen in the Book of Joshua. God had already promised the land of Canaan to the nation of Israel, but He told Joshua, "Every place that the sole of your foot shall tread upon, that have I given unto you, as I said unto Moses" (1:3). In effect, God was saying to Joshua, "I have given the land to you. It is yours, but you must take the step of faith and believe it moment by moment, step by step." Positionally, the land already belonged to Israel, but experientially they had to appropriate what God had promised.

A similar principle is seen in the New Testament. Ephesians 1:3 assures us that God "hath blessed us with all spiritual blessings in heavenly places in Christ." Although the blessings are already ours, we must appropriate them in order to experience the reality. Concerning the matter of having died to sin, it is possible that you might say, "Oh, I really want to die to sin." But you do not need to long to die to sin—you have already died. Your need is to reckon on this fact. Count it as true that, in Christ, you have already died to sin. As a believer, you will never be more dead to sin than you are now. Your need is to appropriate what you already have. The more you appropriate, the more you will experience the life of victory God wants you to have. By His death, Jesus Christ broke the power of sin and Satan that enslaved you. But you will not experience this broken power unless you yield yourself completely to the Lord and, by faith, walk in accordance to the indwelling Holy Spirit.

Sin no longer has the right to control you if you know Christ as Saviour. Romans 6:14 assures every Christian: "For sin shall not have dominion over you: for ye are not under the law, but under grace." As a believer, you need to come to the place of saying, "All right, Lord, I know that in Christ Jesus I died to sin, and in Christ Jesus I have also been made alive. Since this is true, I am now giving myself to follow You." This decision can be spoken of as a crisis when you first come to see this truth, yet it is also to be a daily experience as you yield to the Lord and walk the life of faith in obedience to Him. The believer does not need to struggle for righteousness. He is righteous because of what he has in Jesus Christ. The Lord Jesus Christ is the end of the struggle for righteousness. The believer's need is to reckon on what he has in Christ and then let Christ live out His life through him.

The walk according to the Spirit that Romans 8:4 refers to is a walk that involves taking one step of faith at a time. The believer does not achieve spiritual maturity in one giant step. This comes as he lives a step at a time in dependence on the Holy Spirit. When the believer has a lack of faith and fails in his spiritual walk, he may be assured that God has made provisions for these occasional times when he falls into sin.

The Apostle John instructed believers: "If we walk in the light, as he is in the light, we have fellowship one with another, and the blood of Jesus Christ his Son cleanseth us from all sin" (I John 1:7). In this same passage, the Apostle John wrote: "If we confess our sins, he is faithful and just to forgive us our sins, and to cleanse us from all unrighteousness" (v. 9). How many times will God forgive you? Every time you sin. More than once a day? As many times a day as you sin. Your need is to come to Him and say, "Lord, I have sinned." Be specific and name the sin involved. When you confess to God, trust His promise to forgive you and to cleanse you from all unrighteousness.

182

The Apostle John continued in his first epistle by saying, "My little children, these things write I unto you, that ye sin not" (2:1). The apostle was not opening the door for permissive, loose living by the believers. The purpose of his writing what he did was so they would not sin. However, in case they did sin he wanted to be sure they knew: "If any man sin, we have an advocate with the Father, Jesus Christ the righteous" (v. 2). Jesus Christ is our faithful High Priest. He represents us before the Heavenly Father.

As a result of Christ's death on the cross, provisions have been made for our forgiveness and continual cleansing. Perhaps you have confessed the same sin so many times that you are ashamed of it. Most believers probably feel this way about certain sins that have been special problems in their lives. The more we desire to please God, the more disappointed we are when we stumble in our walk with Him and commit an act of sin—especially if it is the same sin we have committed before. But we need to remember that the Lord understands, and He wants us to keep coming to Him when we sin. The Lord knows what we are like. Psalm 103:13,14 reminds us, "Like as a father pitieth his children, so the Lord pitieth them that fear him. For he knoweth our frame; he remembereth that we are dust." God knows the struggle we have with sin, and in His great love He has made provision for our forgiveness and cleansing.

We should not let Satan overwhelm us with discouragement just because we are imperfect in our Christian walk. No believer has ever lived a perfect life—not even the Apostle Paul. It was Paul's burning desire to know the Lord better. In his epistle to the Philippians he wrote: "That I may know him [Christ], and the power of his resurrection, and the fellowship of his sufferings, being made conformable unto his death" (3:10). But Paul also added, "Not as though I had already attained, either were already perfect: but I follow after, if that I may apprehend that for which also I am apprehended of Christ Jesus. Brethren, I count not myself to have apprehended: but this one thing I do, forgetting those things which are behind, and reaching forth unto those things which are before, I press toward the mark for the prize of the high calling of God in Christ Jesus" (vv. 12-14). Paul was able to forget the past by confessing his sins and trusting God to forgive and cleanse as He had promised. Having done this, Paul pressed on toward maturity in the Christian life, but even he had to live the Christian life a step at a time.

In yielding ourselves to the Lord, we are to yield, not as servants, but as bondservants. The Old Testament instructed: "If thou buy an Hebrew servant, six years he shall serve: and in the seventh he shall go out free for nothing" (Ex. 21:2). However, there was also the stipulation: "If the servant shall plainly say, I love my master, my wife, and my children; I will not go out free: Then his master shall bring him unto the judges; he shall also bring him to the door, or unto the door post; and his master shall bore his ear through with an aul; and he shall serve him for ever" (vv. 5,6). Such a slave was considered a "bondslave" because he willingly bound himself to his master.

In the New Testament, Christians are told, "What? know ye not that your body is the temple of the Holy Ghost which is in you, which ye have of God, and ye are not your own? For ye are bought with a price: therefore glorify God in your body, and in your spirit, which are God's" (I Cor. 6:19,20). By His death on the cross for us, Christ bought us for Himself. As we yield to Him, therefore, we do not yield just as servants but as bondservants. Because of what He has done for us, we willingly serve Him and seek to please Him in all that we do. God does not force us to serve Him against our wills; He wants us to serve Him by choice. He has not made us so that we cannot sin, but He has made it possible for us not to sin if we will completely follow Him in faith.

The believer can never again be brought into the relationship with the sin nature which he had before salvation. This is indicated in Romans 6:9-11: "Knowing that Christ being raised from the dead dieth no more; death hath no more dominion over him. For in that he died, he died unto sin once: but in that he liveth, he liveth unto God. Likewise reckon ye also yourselves to be dead indeed unto sin, but alive unto God through Jesus Christ our Lord." Just as death had no more control over Christ after He died unto sin once, so also the sin nature has no more control over the believer because he has died with Christ.

The believer is a new creation of God: "Therefore if any man be in Christ, he is a new creature [creation]: old things are passed away; behold, all things are become new" (II Cor. 5:17). Because the believer is a new creation in Christ, sin no longer has control over him. From Romans 6:3,4 we see that each believer is a partaker with Christ in His death, burial and resurrection. The believer has died to sin—a fact which he needs to know; he has been buried with Christ—which emphasizes a putting away of the old things; and he has been raised up with Christ—to an entirely different realm of life over which the old nature has no control. It is the believer's responsibility to know these things, to reckon on them, to yield to God, and to walk by faith according to the Holy Spirit.

How to Reckon

There is nothing Satan would like more than to blind the Christian's eyes concerning the truth of how he may have victory in his life. It does not trouble Satan if the Christian has knowledge of the facts as long as the Christian does not apply them to his life. Romans 6:11 says, "Likewise reckon ye also yourselves to be dead indeed unto sin, but alive unto God through Jesus Christ our Lord." Perhaps you have asked yourself, How does reckoning myself dead to sin work out in experience? How does it become reality? The believer's responsibility is to reckon as true that

186

which is true. It is not enough just to know the facts—they must be applied to his life if there is going to be a change in experience.

We are to know that our death with Christ is a historic fact. Romans 6:6 makes this clear when it says, "Knowing this, that our old man is [was] crucified with him, that the body of sin might be destroyed, that henceforth we should not serve sin." We are to reckon this historic fact to be true, just as we reckon it a historic fact that Jesus Christ died on the cross for our sins. Not only did He die for our sins, but we also died with Him to the old nature. If Jesus had not died for our sins there would be no justification. Also, if we had not died with Him to sin, there would be no Christian victory.

As a believer, consider the way you received forgiveness of sins. Did you ask Jesus to come and die for your sins? No, you reckoned on the fact that He had already done this. You considered it so and you thanked Him for it. What is true of the forgiveness of the penalty of sin is also true of the deliverance from the power of sin. "As ye have therefore received Christ Jesus the Lord, so walk ye in him" (Col. 2:6). By faith we are to reckon on the fact that we have died to sin with Christ and the power of sin has been broken.

Many Christians make the mistake of thinking they are to die to the old self now—that they are to be crucified now. But when did Christ die for your sins? He died for your sins nearly 2000 years ago. It was also at that time that you died with Him to

187

sin. Your death to sin is a past fact because the crucifixion of Christ is past. At the very time Christ died for our sins, positionally we died with Him to sin. Therefore, it is not that we are to be presently crucified with Christ, but that we have already been crucified with Him. When the Apostle Paul wrote, "I am crucified with Christ" (Gal. 2:20), he used the past tense, which should literally be translated, "I have been crucified with Christ." We are not dying now with Christ, nor do we look forward to dying with Christ; we died with Him when He died on the cross.

We must also realize that our efforts to make ourselves dead to sin and to self are entirely useless because we are already dead to sin and to self. Perhaps you ask, Why, then, do I have such a problem with sin? It is because sin did not die; it is you that died to sin. The believer has been co-crucified with Christ—separated from the claims and power of sin. Sin is still there, but its power has been broken. However, it will usurp control over the believer whenever it can. It is still *possible* for the believer to yield to sin, but it is no longer *necessary* for him to do so.

Only crucifixion could take care of the sin problem. It was necessary to treat the cause—the sin nature—not just the effects—individual sins. The only way God could give us victory over sin was to separate us from the control of the sin nature. He did not eradicate it nor destroy it, but He made it possible for us to die to it in the death of Christ, thereby breaking its control over us. Since its control has been broken, it is necessary for us to reckon it true by realizing that we no longer need to yield to the power of sin. But even if we do yield to its power, it still remains a fact that we have died to sin and its power over us has been broken. What a shame it is for Christians to live as if the power of sin had never been broken. How spiritually impoverished we become when we yield to its control even though we do not have to. Although the Devil may seek to persuade us that we are still bound by sin's power, we need to realize this is not true because of what was accomplished in the crucifixion of Christ.

Another question is, How does reckoning ourselves to be dead unto sin give us power over sin? As long as we count on our own strength to overcome sin, God cannot work. He shares His glory with no one. But when we count on God alone to do it, He will show His strength. Believers are bankrupt as far as power over self and sin are concerned, so they must count entirely on God by believing what He has already done and trusting Him to work out His power. When we believe what God says is true about our dying to sin, He makes these truths effective in our lives. We must believe that God will do what He has promised.

As the nation of Israel stood before the Red Sea, they had to believe that God would lead them through the sea when He told them to go through. In order for them to experience God's power, they had to trust Him completely and act upon His word.

To experience victory in the Christian life, you must yield to Him and act by faith upon what He has said. You must come to the place of saying, "Lord, I believe that I have died to sin; therefore, I say No to it. I also believe that I am alive to You; therefore, I say Yes to You." If you will do this, God will do the rest. If there is failure, it is not because God has failed—He never fails. It is only when we do not take God at His word that there is failure. When there is failure, our responsibility is to come to the Lord and confess our sins to Him. "If we confess our sins, he is faithful and just to forgive us our sins, and to cleanse us from all unrighteousness" (I John 1:9).

Concerning these important truths, we must always remember that knowing precedes reckoning. To attempt to teach or practice reckoning without knowledge is useless. We have to know what the facts are before we can reckon them to be true. We are not dead to sin because we reckon it to be so, but we are to reckon it so because we are dead to sin. The believer's reckoning is not a reckoning *toward* death but a reckoning *from* death. Having died to sin with Christ, we are now alive unto God.

Having seen from the Scriptures that you have died to sin and have been raised unto newness of life, pray that God will keep these truths before you. Ask Him to enlighten your mind so that you might grasp these truths in greater reality. As you reckon on these things, pray that God will produce the desired results in you and then trust Him to do so. Thank Him for the victory that is in Jesus Christ. As a new creation of God, be aware that "sin shall not have dominion over you: for ye are not under the law, but under grace" (Rom. 6:14).

As you pray concerning these things, be sure to remember your personal responsibility: "Neither yield ye your members as instruments of unrighteousness unto sin: but yield yourselves unto God, as those that are alive from the dead, and your members as instruments of righteousness unto God" (v. 13). Knowing that you have died to sin and that you no longer need to yield to its control, refuse to sin when temptation comes. Say an emphatic No to sin, and yield yourself to God. He will make these truths effective in your life. Because you are not your own, for you have been bought with a price, never yield the members of your body to sin; offer them to God because they are His. Put yourself at God's disposal at all times. Be ready for anything He calls on you to do, trusting Him always to make effective in you what you have trusted Him for.

Do not be discouraged when you realize you cannot attain Christian maturity in one giant step. Satan does not turn loose easily. He will use every conceivable means to seduce you to sin. But always remember James 4:7: "Submit yourselves therefore to God. Resist the devil, and he will flee from you." This resisting must be done on the basis of your identification with Christ. At the cross, Christ overcame the Devil (Heb. 2:14). Because you are now in Christ, by faith you can resist the Devil and he will flee from you. In your growth in the Christian life, remember that a person walks a step at a time. As you walk a step at a time in dependence on God, you will find these truths becoming more and more real in your life.

Jesus said, "If any man will come after me, let him deny himself, and take up his cross daily, and follow me" (Luke 9:23). Notice this is to be a daily practice. Take time in your personal devotions each day to claim the fact that you have died to sin and to self and that you have been made alive unto God. Put yourself at the disposal of the Lord each day, trusting Him to keep you and strengthen you.

Always remember, God has made it possible for you not to sin, but "if any man sin, we have an advocate with the Father, Jesus Christ the righteous" (I John 2:1).